TRUTH
for Your Mind

LOVE
for Your Heart

Satisfying Your Hunger for God

Alfred McBride, O.Praem.

Our Sunday Visitor Publishing Division
Our Sunday Visitor, Inc.
Huntington, Indiana 46750

Nihil Obstat
Msgr. Michael Heintz, Ph.D.
Censor Librorum

Imprimatur
✠ Kevin C. Rhoades
Bishop of Fort Wayne-South Bend
September 28, 2010

Cover design: Lindsey Riesen
Cover art: Shutterstock
Interior design: M. Urgo

PRINTED IN THE UNITED STATES OF AMERICA

I dedicate this book to Bob Lockwood, who was responsible for bringing me to Our Sunday Visitor, and especially for publishing my Scripture books and commentaries on the new Catechism. *I also wish to include in this dedication Jackie Lindsey, who has encouraged me in all my writings for the company, and who has been an inspiring editor. I have been blessed by these good and faithful supporters of Catholic publishing, and I extend my love to Bob and Jackie.*

CONTENTS

SECTION THREE: Satisfying Your Hunger for God

FOREWORD

When asked by the staff of Our Sunday Visitor to write this book connecting doctrine and devotion, I was excited by the challenge to be part of a movement in the Church to do what we can to piece together the strands of Catholic teachings and popular devotion.

I have been writing and teaching about the *Catechism of the Catholic Church* (CCC) since its publication in 1994. And I have found various ways to adapt it for different audiences. This is the first time I needed to link faith teaching and the devotional life of our people. In each of the thirty-four chapters, I attempted to stress the essence of a given teaching with the faith witness of a saint or other outstanding person. The faith lived is the most powerful way to get at the heart of God's Word. I did not intend to give a full catechesis of a topic, but rather pick the core upon which a full explanation might be built.

At the same time, I sought to link the teaching with the spiritual and moral life of the readers of this book. Each chapter attempts to do that in various ways, such as reflections that apply the teaching to the reader, as well as prayers, questions, and meditations that achieve the same goal. I believe that popular piety is a powerful way to open our minds and hearts to the revealed Word of God in Scripture, and above all in the New Testament revelation of Jesus Christ, the Word made flesh who dwelt among us.

I have long believed that the lives of saints and other outstanding witnesses to Christ are as persuasive as any abstract explanations, essential as they are. I suggest that the conversion of Thomas Merton from secularity to Christianity illustrates the human capacity for God even in unpromising circumstances.

I found a remarkable witness of faith in the life of a poor young Austrian farmer, Franz Jägerstätter, who stood up to the Nazis and died for what he believed. When wondering how to bring the issues of Scripture and Tradition alive, I turned to the remarkable story of St. Jerome, who single-handedly created a popular Latin translation of the whole Bible, a work that nourished the devotion of believers for over fifteen hundred years.

Sometimes a world-famous picture helps me to open up the beautiful teaching that we are images of God. I have described Michelangelo's fresco on the ceiling of the Sistine Chapel that captures the instant when God created Adam. We see God as a burly father figure reaching out with his creative index finger to transform the limp body of Adam into a pulsating human being made in God's image.

When I came to the all-too-familiar redemption story of the Passion and Resurrection of Christ, I needed an example of an evangelizer who tirelessly preached the Paschal Mystery. Who else would I choose but Pope John Paul II, in one of his greatest evangelizing events, the 1993 World Youth Day in Denver, Colorado? The state had never seen anything like it. Prophets of gloom predicted it would be a fiasco. Yet the final Mass, celebrated against the backdrop of the mighty Rockies and finishing as the setting sun framed the peaks, was attended by the biggest crowd in the state's history. It was more than a Passion play; it was the age-old sacrament of death and resurrection.

How would I find a way to lead readers into the contemplative life and times of our Holy Mother Mary? I had visited the House of Mary, situated on a cliff overlooking the ruins of the classical city of Ephesus in Turkey. I imagined her living there with St. John and devoting her contemplative prayer to enrich John as he wrote his mystical Gospel. I also noted her powerful prayer for St. Paul, who was a missionary in Ephesus for two years. Was she not already the "Star of Evangelization"? Even more, she could look down at the city and see the prominent, white marble building near the canal wharf. I thought of how that building became the Church of Mary, where the Council of Ephesus was held in 431, and of the decision by the bishops to declare Mary as *Theotokos* ("God-bearer"), the Mother of God. Now, every New Year's Day celebrates this feast of Mary and recalls the city where she spent her last years on earth.

The long imprisonment of Vietnamese Bishop Francis Xavier Van Thuan and the story of how he persuaded his guards to provide him with some bread and wine each month, which he secretly used for a daily Eucharist, seemed to me to be a great introduction to the sacraments, especially the Eucharist.

Being a Norbertine, I could not avoid the story of St. Norbert, whom Church tradition named an "Apostle of the Blessed Sacrament," because of his defense of the Real Presence against its denial in his times. So important is this sacrament that I devoted two chapters to it, one for Holy Thursday and our devotion to the Mass, and the other to the feast of Corpus Christi and the joy of adoration.

To draw the reader into the mystery of a living God, amid the resurgence of popular atheism, I judged that the conversion story of C. S. Lewis from atheist to a believer in God and becoming a Christian would be a good way to strengthen our belief in God as asked by the First Commandment. His defense of Christianity and the reality of

God has strengthened the faith and belief of thousands of people in countless ways.

Isaiah's vision of the holiness of God is a perfect way of motivating a devotion to the Holy Name of God.

A sermon by Pope Benedict XVI at the Eucharistic Congress in Bari, Italy, seemed a most suitable introduction to "Keep Holy the Sabbath," in a period when Sunday worship has declined.

The list goes on. I found a story of a father nourishing his son's self-respect for the development of a strong family for a strong culture. For the Fifth Commandment, the conversion of Bernard Nathanson from abortionist to pro-life defender to his baptism by Cardinal John O'Connor at St. Patrick's Cathedral sets the stage for "The Dignity of Life" as our answer to the culture of death. For the Sixth and Ninth Commandments, the inspiring lives of Louis and Zélie Martin, parents of St. Thérèse of Lisieux, show the real meaning of these commandments — namely, fidelity. Archbishop Oscar Romero's courageous defense of the poor that led to his martyrdom while raising the chalice at Mass does more to teach the value of a social conscience than any number of words.

I wanted to end this book with a tribute to Holy Mary, our Holy Mother. The story of St. Catherine Labouré and the Miraculous Medal and the doctrine of Mary's Immaculate Conception brings together some of the strands of doctrine and devotion. After several centuries of dividing religion into specialties — such as moral theology, Scripture scholarship, liturgical history and practice, canon law, systematic theology, and devotional practice — there is a hunger for integration. In these few pages, some progress of this kind, in a most limited sense, can be done. It will take a lot of time and the commitment of the Church's talented scholars in the years ahead. May God bless them.

In closing, I wish to thank Bert Ghezzi and Patty Mitchell for recommending my manuscript to Our Sunday Visitor for publication. I also appreciate the approval of the publisher, Greg Erlandson, as well as Jackie Lindsey and other staff members who made this possible. And, finally, I am grateful to Woodeene Koenig-Bricker for her expert editing of the text. May the warm embrace of our Holy Mother Mary and the fire of Jesus in the Holy Eucharist touch your hearts and deepen your faith.

FATHER ALFRED MCBRIDE, O.PRAEM.
St. Joseph Priory
De Pere, Wisconsin

— TO GOD ALONE BE THE GLORY —

SECTION ONE

TRUTH FOR YOUR MIND

CHAPTER ONE

THE UNIVERSAL THIRST FOR GOD

O God, you are my God, I seek you,
my soul thirsts for you;
my flesh faints for you. — PSALM 63:1

When he was still in his early twenties, Thomas Merton (1915-1968), an intensely active and brilliant young man, found that nothing in his worldly life satisfied his growing restlessness. A curiosity about religious matters aroused by the writings of the philosopher Étienne Gilson and the poetry of the Jesuit priest Gerard Manley Hopkins led him to become a Catholic and finally to enter the Trappist Abbey of Gethsemane in Kentucky. It was there that he wrote *The Seven Storey Mountain*, an account of his spiritual journey.

In it, Merton writes how, during his trip to Rome in the 1930s, he was surprised that he was more inspired by the art and architecture of churches than by the temples of Imperial Rome:

I found myself looking into churches rather than ruined temples. After the boring, semi-pornographic statuary of empire, what a thing it was to come upon the genius of an art full of spiritual vitality.

I was fascinated by these Byzantine mosaics. These mosaics and frescoes and all the ancient altars and thrones were built for the instruction of people. I began to find out something of who this person was, that was called Christ. The saints of those forgotten days had left upon the walls of their churches words which by the peculiar grace of God I was able in some measure to comprehend. I could not help but catch the ancient craftsman's love of Christ the redeemer and judge of the world.[1]

"You have made us for yourself,
O Lord, and our heart is restless until it
rests in you."

— St. Augustine

Merton's life story is a journey from a world of inner restlessness without God to one in which "God alone" satisfied his soul. His path began with beauty and art as he first found it in the old churches of Rome. Eventually, he met people of faith who led him to the Catholic Church and finally to a life of contemplation at Gethsemane Abbey. Merton's life illustrates our belief as expressed in the *Catechism of the Catholic Church*: "The desire for God is written in the human heart, because man is created by God and for God" (CCC, 27).

Today, like most thoughtful people, we realize our limits in hundreds of ways, yet somehow we are unlimited in our desire for a higher life. We face an abundance of choices but cannot have them all. Painfully we do what we detest, and do not do what we should desire. We live with inner conflict and struggle.

This inner division leads to basic questions: Who am I? How can I explain the suffering, death, and evil that endure despite all modern progress? What can I contribute to my family and country? What should my contribution do for me? Is there really life after death?

In looking for answers to these questions, people throughout the ages have been gradually led to seek God and come to know him.

This search is part of our very being. In his sermon to the Athenians, St. Paul explained that God arranged the order of creation so that people "would search for God and perhaps grope for him and find him — though indeed he is not far from each one of us" (Acts 17:27). Later on, St. Paul wrote to the Romans that the invisible reality of God can be known through the visible things of creation: "Ever since the creation of the world his eternal power and divine nature, invisible though they are, have been understood and seen through the things he has made. So they are without excuse" (Romans 1:20).

Today, we also can move toward God through our interpersonal relationships. Through meeting people, loving them or colliding with them, we learn a lot about ourselves. Love and betrayal, forgiveness and hatred, self-sacrifice and utter selfishness are among our experiences of others and of ourselves. Human relationships run the gamut of shallowness to luminous depth. Human relationships are either lighthouses of God's presence that attract us to him or shadows of evil that push us to run for the nearest exit to evade him.

Through our dialogue with others, we discern our openness to truth and beauty. We observe our capacity for moral goodness. We experience our love of freedom and the voice of conscience. We discover our thirst for the infinite and ultimate happiness. These are ways that convince us of the reality that our souls contain the seeds of eternity, a gift that could only have come from God.

In spite of these paths, we can forget, avoid, or reject these invitations to meet our Lord. Why does this happen? Sometimes we are depressed by the evil in the world and simply give up the quest. Other times we are disillusioned by the scandal given by believers or the cultural disdain for religion. In other instances, sinfulness weakens our capacity to seek God. Yet God never ceases to look for us and call us to seek him and receive the joy he offers.

Millions of people have not yet come to know Christ or the benefits of belonging to the Body of Christ. Through the example of our lives and a commitment to growth in our faith, we enable others who are searching for God to find him. Every Catholic is called to be part of the mission of Christ and the Church. A dynamic Church is essentially a missionary community. A committed Catholic is basically a missionary for the faith.

Each day we need to thank and praise God for the gift of our Catholic faith. We benefit more from this gift by continuing conversion to Christ and being active in the prayer life, liturgy, and charitable endeavors of our parish or religious community to which we belong. A love of the Eucharist is central to our lifelong conversion, and a devotion to Mary assures our dedication to Jesus. As we grow in holiness, so also does the Body of Christ, the Church, become enriched by the graces we receive.

When our souls are fed regularly, we will have a passion for helping others to come to Christ, for the good news in our hearts moves us to share this with others.

Christian Love

Searchers for God in the early Church said, "See how these Christians love one another." The seekers also beheld the incredible courage of so many Christians who died for Christ rather than abandon their faith. Their blood became the seed of new Christians. Pope Paul VI has written, " 'Modern man listens more willingly to witnesses than to teachers, and if he does listen to teachers, it is because they are witnesses' (Pope Paul VI, Address to the Members of the Consilium de Laicis [October 2, 1974]) .... It is therefore primarily by her conduct and by her life that the Church will evangelize the world, in other words, by her living witness of fidelity to the Lord Jesus."[2]

For Reflection

1. Do you know someone who has joined the Church without previous religious affiliation? How did their attraction to the faith begin?
2. How can you help seekers come to our Catholic community of faith? Where are you liable to meet such seekers? at work? at parties? in sports?
3. Besides the power of your personal witness, what might you do to attract a person to the faith?

Prayer

Let us pray
for those who do not believe in God,

that they may find him
by sincerely following all that is right.

Almighty and eternal God,
you created mankind
so that all might long to find you
and have peace when you are found.
Grant that, in spite of the hurtful things
that stand in their way,
they may all recognize in the lives of Christians
the tokens of your love and mercy,
and gladly acknowledge you
as the one true God and Father of us all.
We ask this through Christ our Lord. Amen.

— FROM THE LITURGY OF GOOD FRIDAY
OF THE LORD'S PASSION

CHAPTER TWO

GOD INVITES US TO A LOVE RELATIONSHIP

> *"For God so loved the world that he gave his only Son, so that everyone who believes in him may not perish but may have eternal life."* — JOHN 3:16

While all of us are born with a yearning for God, it is equally true that God wants to be in a loving relationship with us. Sometimes that invitation comes in an extraordinary manner. Take Saul of Tarsus. In his hometown, where he learned to make fine tents from rough strands of goat hair, Saul learned Greek and Latin. His parents sent him to Palestine to study Hebrew and become a rabbi under the instruction of the famed, levelheaded Gameliel. Saul was brilliant, passionate, and fiercely opposed to the new Christian sect.

Saul stood by and guarded the cloaks of the men who stoned Deacon Stephen to death. He approved the arrest and imprisonment of Christians, and he oversaw raids on their homes. He used religion to justify his cruelty. But God had other plans for Saul. On a trip to Damascus for another raid, he was struck to the ground by a blinding light. He heard a voice that said, "Saul, Saul, why do you persecute me?" Saul replied, "Who are you, Lord?" The reply came, "I am Jesus, whom you are persecuting" (Acts 9:4-5).

Christ revealed to Saul that the Christian Church was the Body of Christ. Saul was temporarily blinded until the Lord directed the disciple Ananias to visit Saul. Ananias baptized Saul and restored his sight. Later, God granted Saul, now known as Paul, a revelation of the glory of heaven. Lastly, when Paul wanted God to release him from a "thorn" in his flesh, God said simply: "My grace is sufficient for you" (2 Corinthians 12:9).

It was amid these three revelations — a blinding light, a vision of heaven, and God's Word — that Paul was drenched with the love of Christ. So astonishing was that divine-love relationship that Paul was moved to write the greatest poem on love in the Bible: 1 Corinthians 13:1-13.

Where there is vision there is mission. Paul roamed the Roman Empire, planting churches, preaching Christ, and writing unforgettable pastoral letters. God's revelations were the key to Paul's mission to convert the world to Christ.

"Long ago God spoke to our ancestors in many and various ways by the prophets, but in these last days he has spoken to us by a Son, whom he appointed heir of all things, through whom he also created the worlds."

— HEBREWS 1:1-2

In the Garden of Eden, God met with Adam and Eve and walked with them as a friend. In the ages after the fall of our first parents, God sought out certain people and revealed to them his plan to save us. Eucharistic Prayer IV states that again and again God made new covenants with us. As we say in the Nicene Creed each Sunday: "We believe in the Holy Spirit.... He has spoken through the prophets."

Although through our reason we could find God, we needed to know a great deal more about God, who alone could tell us about himself and about his plans to save us from our sins and give us a share in his life. God took the initiative and formed his own people by calling Abraham to respond in faith and be the founding father of a nation.

Like a loving shepherd, God guided his people through the patriarchs, judges, kings, prophets, and wisdom speakers toward a fulfillment that would occur when the Messiah appeared. Certain writers such as Moses and the prophets recorded the revelations of God. This was the Word of God written in the words of man.

However, the greatest and most complete revelation of God occurred in the incarnation of his Son, Jesus Christ. St. John of the Cross eloquently described this truth about Jesus: "Once he has given us his Son, who is his Word, God has no other word to give us. He has said everything to us, all summed up in that unique Word. What he said partially in the prophets he has said entirely in his Son."[3]

God's revelation tells us truths we could never know by the light of reason alone. Through that revelation, we learn that God is a Trinity of Persons. We are taught that the Son of God became a man to save us. We become aware of the graces received in the seven sacraments by which we are sanctified and transformed into the likeness of Christ. We receive the good news that we are adopted sons and daughters of God through our baptism and reception into the life of the Church.

In the Creation stories in the Book of Genesis, God gave Adam charge of the garden and told him to cultivate it. But God intended more than that, for he loved Adam and Eve and offered them a fruitful relationship based on obedience to his wise direction for their happiness. As we all know, that fateful couple rebelled against God and lost paradise. But as we know from the history of salvation and Christ's redeeming work, God then devised his long-range plan to save us.

In the past two or three centuries, the teaching of God's revelation and his desire to have a love relationship with us have been dampened by a powerful cultural movement that has rejected this truth. Deism promoted the idea that God created the world but left it to us to care for it. This philosophy would have us believe that God is no longer providentially involved in the world or with its people. By shutting the doors to truth, deism opposed the real nature of religion, a word based on the Latin *relegate* (to bind). Religion is more than ideas about God. Religion is a relationship that binds us to God through a bond of love.

Far from leaving us alone, however, God continues to reach out, to wake us up to truths of faith that either are under attack or that we have forgotten. For instance, in the seventeenth century, a French mystic, St. Margaret Mary, received a private revelation from Jesus, who revealed to her his Sacred Heart, pierced on the cross, as a powerful sign of his love for us. Devotion to the Sacred Heart gave Catholics the spiritual energy and holy wisdom to counter the errors of the rationalism that soon arose in the appearance of deism. Since then, on the First Friday of each month, Catholics go to Mass to be fed by the Eucharist. Millions affirm that love and truth when they pray, "Sacred Heart of Jesus, I place my trust in you." (Of course, the Church also employed the strength of reason in the service of faith, while popular piety contributed the spiritual conviction.)

In our own time, the idea of deism has become more radical and is now known in public life as secularism, while its twin in intellectual life is known as relativism. These philosophies reject the sacred and the idea that truth can be known. They claim there is no truth, only opinion. For us as Catholic believers, this would mean that the certitudes of faith — God, the Church, Scripture, the sacraments, a morality based on standards — are simply our opinion and not objectively true. In other words, they are merely an illusion. Unhappily, this way of thinking has affected many members of our Church. Their trust in the truths of revelation has waned. They pick and choose what they prefer to believe. Their commitment to regular weekly worship has declined. Their faith is not being fed and their souls languish, exiled from the Eucharist.

However, love never truly forgets the truth of the beloved. Just as St. Margaret Mary "remembered" in her day, in our time a Polish mystic from Kraków, Poland, St. Faustina Kowalska (1905-1938) received a private revelation of Christ, who revealed to her the power of his Divine Mercy and requested that she have a painting made of her vision showing him pointing to his heart, from which rays of love pour forth, with the prayer "Jesus, I trust in you" at the bottom. His message is that of the Gospels: "Come to me, all you that are weary and are carrying heavy burdens, and I will give you rest.... I will never take back my love; my truth will never fail" (Matthew 11:28; Psalm 89:34[4]).

God always wants to have a relationship with us. By creating and maintaining a relationship with Christ, we learn that love is the golden road to truth and that Divine Mercy is the golden gate to truth. Love and mercy are the foundations of a lasting relationship with God.

Divine Mercy Sunday

Pope John Paul II's legacy includes proclaiming the first Sunday after Easter as Divine Mercy Sunday. He told us that mercy is the second name for the love of God. He said that our strongest response to secularism is the mercy of God that powerfully touches hearts, entering them under their radar to awaken them to faith. Our faith should convince us that wherever the Lord is, there is mercy and truth. The face of Christ is the face of God, a face of mercy. In the Gospels, sinners were attracted to Jesus, who loved to show them mercy. On the cross, Jesus poured out mercy on those who mocked and cursed him, and on the repentant thief. His mercy was sunshine in the darkness of Calvary.

For Reflection

1. How is mercy and forgiveness a priority for you?
2. In what ways must knowledge about God be linked to a loving relationship with him?
3. Why was it necessary for God to reveal himself to us?

Prayer

The Chaplet of Divine Mercy is one of our strongest responses to secularism and relativism. It is said as follows:

- ◆ **Step One:** Using the rosary beads, begin with the Sign of the Cross, one Our Father, one Hail Mary, and the Apostles' Creed.

- **Step Two:** On the Our Father beads say: "Eternal Father, I offer you the Body and Blood, Soul and Divinity of your dearly beloved Son, our Lord Jesus Christ, in atonement for our sins and those of the whole world."

- **Step Three:** On the Hail Mary beads say: "For the sake of his sorrowful Passion, have mercy on us and on the whole world." (Repeat Steps Two and Three for the five decades.)

- **Step Four:** Conclude by saying three times: "Holy God, Holy Mighty One, Holy Immortal One, have mercy on us and on the whole world."

CHAPTER THREE

I BELIEVE YOU ARE HERE

"I believe; help my unbelief!"
— MARK 9:24

The path of faith, of belief in our love relationship with God, is blurred by many difficulties. In his parable of the Seed and the Sower (Matthew 13:3-9; Mark 4:3-9; Luke 8:5-8), Jesus outlined the perils facing those who hear the Word of God. The greatest pitfall for faith in our culture is skepticism. It is based on an attitude of suspicion toward religion, authority, and tradition. It questions the claims of churches, the decisions of authority, and the appeals to traditions. It prizes doubt over belief, dissent over acceptance of moral standards, and the current preference of the present over the past. Yet, even in modern times, men and women make the heroic choice of faith over skepticism. Franz Jägerstätter (1907-1943) was one of them.

When the Nazis imposed their will on Austria in the late 1930s, Franz, a poor farmer with a wife and three children, did not collaborate with them and even rejected their family-assistance program and emergency-relief money when a storm battered his little farm. He practiced charity to the poor. He served as a volunteer sexton for his church and refused any donations for his work. He nourished his faith by reading the Bible and other devotional writings.

In 1943, the Nazis tried to draft Franz into their army. People told him to think of his family. Others said he should obey legitimate authority. He said, "I'm not going to say I was just following orders." He was arrested and, after six months in prison, was executed on August 9, 1943. Before he died, Franz wrote to a friend: "Since the death of Christ, almost every century has seen the persecution of Christians; there have always been heroes and martyrs who gave their lives — often in horrible ways — for Christ and their faith. If we hope to reach our goal some day, then we, too, must become heroes of the faith."

Just before Franz's death, a chaplain paid him a visit. Franz told him, "I am completely bound in inner union with the Lord." The chaplain later testified, "Franz lived as a saint and died as a hero."

Today Franz's home is a national museum, and pilgrims flock to his grave. His 94-year-old wife, Francisca, told a visitor, "I thought no one would ever know about him. I hid his letters under my mattress for decades." Franz's faith led him to profound communion with God. He was beatified on October 26, 2007, by Pope Benedict XVI.

There are many fruitful ways to organize our understanding of the meaning of our Catholic faith. We choose here to describe faith from five points of view rooted in the belief that faith is our response to God's revelation:

1. **Faith is my free and personal "yes" to Christ himself, who reveals his love to me and his desire for a permanent relationship with me.** My "yes" is a response to his revelation and a promise to be committed to him. My "yes" is also given to the Father and the Holy Spirit. My "yes" is a consecration of my mind, will, body, and my whole self to the God,

who attracts me with such powerful love. By revelation God approaches me. By faith I come to God. That is not to say that our "yes" will always be easy, but it will always lead us to profound communion with God.

2. **Faith is my free and personal assent to the message of Christ, to all the truths that he taught by his words, deeds, suffering and death and resurrection.** It is a message that includes all of revelation, from the Book of Genesis to the Book of Revelation. The message is the Word of God developed by the Church and entrusted to her wisdom and authoritative interpretation from the time of the apostles to the present day. In faith I commit myself to hear and study the message — and practice it.

3. **Faith flourishes in the community of believers that is the Church.** Faith in Christ is more than a "Jesus and me" matter. He founded a Church to be the custodian of his message, the place where the sacraments are celebrated, the home of love and support for all its members, the source of hope for the poor, the lost, the sinful, and the seekers for God in all the world. The Church is not for lone rangers but for those who are in solidarity with all who need justice, salvation, and God's help.

4. **Faith is a holy gift from God.** Faith comes to us as a grace, a gift from the Holy Spirit. We do not earn faith or create it out of our own efforts and talents. The Holy Spirit plants an attraction to God in our hearts as well as the faith we need to come to God. It is a strong yet gentle impulse that honors our freedom and fills us with gratitude.

5. Faith always involves obedience to the will of God.
In scriptural culture, the term "obedience" implied more than hearing God's Word; it also included doing what was asked. In the Our Father, Jesus teaches us to say: "Thy will be done." He expects us to mean what we say, and to do what it means.

As we strive to walk the path of faith, we have "a cloud of witnesses" to encourage us — the saints. Pope Benedict XVI's Wednesday talks often center on the lives of the saints as heroes and heroines of faith, and as living examples of Gospel teachings and great ways to push back doubt and skepticism. He has been fighting the culture wars for a long time and has a special interest in skepticism because it erodes people's faith in God and the mysteries of Christ. Benedict has fashioned deep theological arguments against this prevalence of doubt and is a champion of reason in defending the faith; but as a son of the ancient Catholic culture of Bavaria, he grew up with the saints and knows firsthand the effectiveness of their stories of faith.

Cardinal Newman's Secret

Cardinal John Henry Newman (1801-1890) understood the struggles we often have with faith and concluded that a thousand difficulties need not produce one doubt. His *Parochial and Plain Sermons* brilliantly retells the essentials of the faith like a reborn, ancient Father of the Church. Steeped in Scripture and the liturgical year, and supported by amazing insight into human nature, his sermons shed light for us in our current effort to witness to the faith.

Devotion to the saints has been a universal practice in the Church. The ancient Litany of the Saints is sung at every ordination. Baptism confirms the identity of the baptized with a saint's name in the hope that the saint will look after the new Christian and intercede for his or her needs. The saint's life inspires the baptized to grow in faith in God.

Every Catholic church and chapel is named either after Christ, Mary (or an event or doctrine intimately associated with them, such as the Resurrection or the Annunciation), or a saint. Catholics assume that the patronal saint of their parish is a special protector of the parishioners and one who talks to God for their needs. The doctrine of the Communion of Saints is a perfect reason for devotion to the saints and another armor against skeptics.

For Reflection

1. In what ways have you personally experienced doubt?
2. How has your faith helped you oppose and reject doubt when it has crept in?
3. What most helps you combat skepticism?

Prayer

O my God, I firmly believe that you are one God in three divine Persons, Father, Son, and Holy Spirit. I believe that your divine Son became man and died for our sins and that he will come again to judge the living and the dead. I believe these and all the truths which the Holy Catholic Church teaches because you have revealed them who can neither deceive nor be deceived. Amen.

— ACT OF FAITH

CHAPTER FOUR

HOLY WORD AND HOLY TRADITION

> *Tradition and Sacred Scripture are bound closely together and communicate one with the other. Each of them makes present and fruitful in the Church the mystery of Christ. They flow out of the same divine well-spring and together make up one sacred deposit of faith from which the Church derives her certainty about revelation. — COMPENDIUM OF THE CATECHISM OF THE CATHOLIC CHURCH (COMPENDIUM), 14*

All of us owe a great debt to St. Jerome (c. 340-420), who provided a Latin translation of the entire Bible that served the Western Church for 1,500 years. Born in the Balkan Peninsula, his early education gave him mastery of Greek and Latin. Baptized at age 18, he gradually matured in his Catholic faith during a four-year stay at a desert monastery near Antioch. It was there that he also acquired knowledge of Hebrew from a monk who had converted from Judaism. Then he moved to Constantinople, where he received further training in Scripture from a Father of the Eastern Church, St. Gregory Nazianzen.

After Jerome's ordination to the priesthood, he traveled to Rome, where he met Pope Damascus I, who appointed him to write a new and more accurate Latin translation of the Bible. While in Rome, he gained a view of the universal Church and an appreciation of the role of the successor of St. Peter. He also became a spiritual director for a group of devout, wealthy Roman women: Paula, Marcella and Eustochia.

After the pope's death, Jerome moved to Bethlehem, where he devoted all his energies to complete his epic translation of Scripture. He learned more about biblical Hebrew and Aramaic from local rabbis, for whom these were living languages, and their wisdom improved his translating skills. His prosperous women friends migrated to Bethlehem and built a monastery there. Year after year he labored to produce a faithful translation of God's Word. His faith in the power of Scripture moved him to write, "Ignorance of Scripture is ignorance of Christ." On September 30, 1452 — 1,032 years after Jerome's death — the first book printed from movable type was published by Johann Gutenberg in Germany. And what text of the Bible did he publish? Why, the Latin text of Jerome, of course.

Every day the Church reads from Scripture, the Holy Word, at the Eucharist and in her Liturgy of the Hours. In the context of worship, the Church always sings the psalms from God's Prayer Book and reads the teachings of Jesus. In this model, Scripture — God's Word — occupies an essential place in an environment of prayer and adoration of God. The Bible is enshrined in our most sacred daily acts. The Holy Word carries us to the Holy Eucharist, which sheds divine light on our understanding of the Word.

In this view, the liturgy is the school of prayer, permeated by God's Word, exalted by the flame of the Eucharist, ennobled by a faith community, and uplifted by adoration of the living God. Liturgy trains us how to pray Scripture, to treat the Word of God with reverence, and to approach this record of divine revelation with faith.

But Scripture does not stand alone. Holy Tradition — also known as Apostolic Tradition — is the living transmission of the Word of God as preached and witnessed to us by Jesus Christ. Holy Tradition passes on, in its entirety, the Word of God entrusted to the apostles by Christ and the Holy Spirit. The oral preaching of the apostles and the written message of salvation, conserved in Scripture, are handed on to us through apostolic succession in the Church. Tradition and Scripture flow from the single source of revelation of God in Jesus Christ. The Church does not derive its certainty about revealed truths from Scripture alone, but from both Scripture and Tradition.

Jesus called and trained the apostles in the meaning and message of his life, death, resurrection, and sending

The Table of Scripture and the Table of Eucharist

"I acknowledge my need of two things — food and light. You have therefore given me in my weakness Your sacred Body to be the refreshment of my soul and body, and have set Your Word as a lamp to my feet. Without these two I cannot rightly live; for the Word of God is the light of my soul and Your Sacrament is the bread of my life. One might describe them as two tables, set on either side of the treasury of holy Church. The one is the table of the holy altar, having on it the holy bread, the precious Body of Christ. The other is that of the divine law that enshrines the holy doctrine, teaches the true faith, and unerringly guides our steps even within the veil that guards the Holy of Holies."[5]

— THOMAS À KEMPIS

of the Holy Spirit. He gave them the mission to preach the Gospel and baptize those who accept it in faith. He gave them the mystery of the Holy Eucharist and the power to celebrate it. On Easter night, he breathed the Holy Spirit upon them and endowed them with the power to forgive sins in his name. Jesus formed them into the nucleus of his Church under the leadership of Peter and in communion with him.

To make sure that the living Gospel should always be preached and witnessed, the apostles left us bishops, who would have apostolic authority to continue Christ's work as the apostles did. Under the guidance of the apostles and their successors, the life and teachings of Jesus were handed on, first in an oral manner and then by written Gospels. As time passed, three rules for interpreting Scripture developed:

♦ First, we need to uphold the unity of Scripture. The diverse books are united by God's plan of salvation — in which Jesus is the center — all the way from Genesis to Revelation.

♦ Second, we should read Scripture within the living Tradition of the whole Church, from apostolic times to the present, remembering all of the profound insights given by the Holy Spirit to the saints and scholars.

♦ Third, we should read Scripture with the analogy of faith, which affirms the coherence of the truths it contains and in the light of God's plan to save us. The Magisterium of the Church, the Church's teaching authority, gives us a sure guide to the truths we receive from Holy Tradition and Holy Scripture.

Some approaches to the interpretation of Scripture undermine the reliability of the texts, doubting the truth of the Gospels and the historical accuracy of the material. Others deny the objective reality of Jesus and urge us simply to rely on our personal feelings, treating the texts as little more than a form of inspirational poetry. Behind all this is the separation of faith from scholarship. The result is confusion, loss of trust in Scripture, and gnawing doubt about its reliability.

Dancing With the Torah

Chaim Potok's description of the "Dance of the Torah" helps raise an awareness of the Bible as a book in which God speaks to us, inviting us to a relationship, instead of just a book about God. The scene is a Hasidic synagogue in the Williamsburg section of Brooklyn. A religious festival is in progress, and the participants are passing around the scrolls of the Torah (the first five books of the Bible) to privileged members who are allowed to dance with it. We pick up the scene where the principal character, who has been agonizing about his faith, is handed the scroll: "I held the scroll as something precious to me, a living being with whose soul I was forever bound, this Sacred Scroll, the Word, this Fire of God, this source for my own creation, this velvet encased Fountain of All Life, which I now clasped in a passionate embrace. I danced with the Torah for a long time, following the line of dancers through the steamy air of the synagogue and out into the chill tumultuous street and back into the synagogue and then reluctantly yielding the scroll to a huge dark-bearded man who hungrily scooped it up and swept away with it in his arms."[6]

A balanced, faith-informed, and reasonable refutation of these views is given by Pope Benedict XVI in the fore-word of his book *Jesus of Nazareth*. He supports the legitimate conclusions of the historical-critical method, while citing its limitations. He also insists on the Church's traditional teachings about Scripture as God's Word — inspired by the Holy Spirit, requiring faith by the reader — and the other concepts cited at the beginning of this chapter. He writes, "The main implication of this for my portrayal of Jesus is that I trust the Gospels."[7]

Holy Tradition protects us from wandering too far from the authentic meaning of the Holy Word. That is what makes the daily Eucharist and Liturgy of the Hours central to helping us pray the texts with confidence in their ability to guide us in our spiritual and moral growth, as well as being transformed into Christ.

For Reflection

1. What helps you to read Scripture prayerfully?
2. In what ways does Holy Tradition give you confidence in your faith?
3. How does liturgy help you understand the Bible?

Prayer

O Lord Jesus Christ, open Thou the eyes of my heart, that I may hear Thy word and understand and do Thy will, for I am a sojourner upon the earth. Hide not Thy commandments from me, but open mine eyes, that I may perceive the wonders of Thy law. Speak unto me the hidden and secret things of Thy wisdom. On Thee do I set my hope, O my God, that Thou shalt enlighten my mind and understanding with the light of Thy knowledge, not only to cherish those things which are written, but to do them; that in reading the lives and sayings of the saints I may not sin, but that such may serve for my restoration, enlightenment, and sanctification, for the salvation of my soul, and the inheritance of life everlasting. For Thou art the enlightenment of those who lie in darkness, and from Thee cometh every good deed and every gift. Amen.

— St. John Chrysostom, Prayer Before Reading or Listening to the Word of God

CHAPTER FIVE

LOVE GOD WITH ALL YOUR HEART

> *"You shall love the Lord your God with all your heart, and with all your soul, and with all your strength, and with all your mind." —* LUKE 10:27

At the canonization of Edith Stein (1891-1942), Pope John Paul II said: "She discovered that truth had a name: Jesus Christ. From that moment on, the Incarnate Word was her One and All.… She wrote to a Benedictine nun, 'Whoever seeks the truth is seeking God, whether consciously or unconsciously.' … At the end of a long journey she came to the surprising realization: only those who commit themselves to the love of Christ become truly free."[8]

Edith was born on the Jewish Day of Atonement in 1891 in Breslau, Germany. The youngest of eleven children, she was raised in a devout Jewish family. Edith said that at age 14 she had consciously and deliberately stopped praying. Relying exclusively on herself, she pursued personal freedom and chose atheism.

Gifted with a brilliant mind and acclaimed as a professional philosopher, Edith never tired of searching for the truth. At age 29, after reading the *Autobiography of St. Teresa of Ávila* in one sitting, she found the truth and joined the Catholic Church.

At age 42, Edith became a Carmelite nun in Cologne and took the name Sister Teresa Benedict of the Cross.

Eventually, her sister Rosa joined her. After the terror of *Kristallnacht*, for their safety Sister Teresa Benedict and Rosa moved secretly to the Carmel in Echt, Holland. When the Nazis conquered Holland, they were again in danger. All Jewish people (including Catholic converts) in Echt, Holland, were rounded up and sent to the death camps. Sister Teresa Benedict and Rosa were taken to Auschwitz, where they were executed in 1942. Edith Stein was canonized St. Teresa Benedict of the Cross on October 11, 1998.

Edith Stein's journey to faith in God and membership in the Church grew from the seeds of belief planted in her heart by her devout mother. Like many others today, Edith abandoned her ancestral religion and joined a generation of seekers. It was her good fortune to be blessed with a philosophical mind and an eminent teacher, Edmund Husserl. She felt the inner drive to know the truth and never gave up until she found it.

C. S. Lewis underwent a similar process. A cradle Protestant, he left his faith as a teenager and became an atheist. Trained at Oxford in the classics and medieval literature, he became a brilliant tutor, lecturer, and author. He was blessed by making friends with several Oxford professors who were practicing Christians, especially J. R. R. Tolkien, a Catholic and author of *The Lord of the Rings*. Meeting once a week at a pub, where they critiqued one another's writings, Lewis found himself touched by his friends' faith. After a time, Lewis found himself once again believing in God. Then one summer evening, sitting alone in his room, he experienced a joy so profound that he spontaneously knelt down as "the most reluctant convert [to Christianity] in all England."

These conversion stories matter to us, first, because they occurred in modern times among elite who were not inclined to favor Christianity and who often ridiculed those who made a choice to believe. Second, their faith endured and they lived it. Edith Stein became a Carmelite nun and "a martyr of love." Lewis applied his remarkable writing talent to become an outstanding defender of Christianity. While he never became a Catholic — probably due to his Ulster upbringing that bred resistance to Catholicism — his writings have drawn many to join our Church.

What these converts, indeed all of us, have in common is our belief in the essentials of the faith. From the

The Creed of Israel

One of the greatest creedal statements in the Old Testament is in Deuteronomy 6:4-5: "Hear, O Israel: The Lord is our God, the LORD alone. You shall love the LORD your God with all your heart, and with all your soul, and with all your might." The inspired text calls us to listen, to hear God's Word. God asks us to profess our belief in him and to practice our faith by loving him with all our heart, soul, and strength. God's Word binds faith and love into one powerful commitment. Faith and love form the seamless garment of our religion.

Creeds are more than statements about God; they are calls to consecration of self, dedication to the divine, willingness to take the risk of being a believer, readiness to embark on an adventure that is the consequence of surrendering to God's plans for us. Edith Stein died for her faith; C. S. Lewis bore the scorn of many in the academic community for his defense of Christianity.

earliest days of Christianity, an effort was made to summarize these beliefs, especially for those to be baptized. These professions of faith were first fashioned into the Apostles' Creed and used by candidates for baptism in the Church at Rome. St. Cyril of Jerusalem noted, "This summary of faith encompassed in a few words the whole knowledge of the true religion contained in the Old and New Testaments."

These creeds, or professions of faith, enable us to enrich our knowledge of God, especially his loving plan to save us from sin and share his life with us. But before we can confess our faith with our lips, we must experience it in our hearts.

We can do a number of things to make more room in our hearts for God's presence:

1. **Seek humility first.** If you feel stuck in your spiritual search for God, seek humility instead. Pride is one of the most effective ways to block God from our lives. True humility is not the same as low self-esteem or thinking you are bad. Read the story of Moses who was known as "a very humble man, more humble than anyone else on the face of the earth," to help understand the difference.

2. **Go on a cynicism fast.** Commit yourself to a period of time when you will refrain from indulging in all sources of cynicism. Give up TV shows and reading websites that make jokes at other people's expense (even about celebrities and politicians). Avoid making cynical jokes. You will be surprised how effective this fast will be.

3. **Read the great Christian authors.** Seeking God does not mean setting aside logic and reason. Asking tough questions and hearing the answers of great Christian thinkers will bring you closer to God. Read G. K. Chesterton's *Orthodoxy*, Augustine's *Confessions*, and C. S. Lewis' *Mere Christianity*.

4. **Do the experiment.** I believe that God's existence can be proven in a certain sense as long as you understand that God is Love and that what you're trying to prove is Love itself. This is not something you can know from analyzing data or reading books alone. To get the proof you seek, you must enter the laboratory of your heart. Live for a while as though God did exist. Follow the Ten Commandments. Show love and kindness to everyone, even your enemies. Read the Bible. Give God the thanks, love, and respect you would show him if he did exist. Try this for a while. See what happens.

5. **Pray frequently.** This is the most important step. You may feel like you are talking to yourself. You don't see the point of it. But there is no substitute for humbly, regularly turning toward God with an open mind and open heart. If you don't know what to say, just pray: "God I want to find you. Show me how. I'm listening."

For Reflection

1. Why do people, especially the young, stop practicing their faith?
2. What misunderstandings about God exist today?
3. How can you be a daily witness to God's love?

Prayer

God our Father, life of the faithful, glory of the humble, happiness of the just, hear the prayer of your children. Fill our emptiness with your divine presence. We ask this through your Son, our Lord, in union with your Holy Spirit. Amen.

— ADAPTED FROM THE OPENING PRAYER FOR WEDNESDAY OF
THE FOURTH WEEK OF EASTER

CHAPTER SIX

"BATTER MY HEART, THREE PERSON'D GOD"

> *The Church expresses her trinitarian faith by professing a belief in the oneness of God in whom there are three Persons: Father, Son, and Holy Spirit. The three divine Persons are only one God because each of them equally possesses the fullness of the one and indivisible divine nature.... Inseparable in their one substance, the three divine Persons are also inseparable in their activity.* — COMPENDIUM, 48-49

In the third century, Arius, a priest in Alexandria, Egypt, began preaching that Jesus was not the divine Son of God. The consequence of this teaching was that if Jesus was not the divine Son of God, then the doctrine of the Trinity was also untrue. St. Athanasius (295-373), who was later named a Doctor of the Church, lived during this time.

Athanasius was born and raised in Alexandria at a time when it was the largest seaport in the world. He was given an excellent education and was ordained a deacon at age 21.

In 325, the emperor Constantine called the Council at Nicaea for the purpose of resolving the dispute caused by Arius and restoring unity to the Church. Athanasius attended the council as secretary to his bishop, Alexander. (While the council upheld the traditional teaching about

Christ's divinity and the Holy Trinity, its acceptance was later diluted by certain bishops and some emperors.)

Upon Alexander's death in 328, Athanasius was named bishop of Alexandria and became an ardent and

Jesus Reveals the Trinity

We must never forget that it is Jesus who reveals the Trinity to us. In the Old Testament, the term "Father" (for God) appears occasionally, but in the New Testament it is used by Jesus 170 times. He revealed his intimacy with the Father, not just by closeness, but also by identity: "Believe me that I am in the Father and the Father is in me" (John 14:11).

Moreover, Jesus prophesied the existence and the role of the Holy Spirit in the divine family: "When the Spirit of truth comes, he will guide you into all truth. . . . He will glorify me, because he will take what is mine and declare it to you" (John 16:13, 14). At Christ's baptism, the Father acknowledged his Son and the Spirit confirmed this under the appearance of a dove; at the Transfiguration, the Father again acknowledged his relationship to his Son and the Spirit confirmed this under the appearance of the shining cloud. Christ's final words to the apostles just before his ascension included a specific reference to the Holy Trinity: "And Jesus came and said to them, 'All authority in heaven and on earth has been given to me. Go therefore and make disciples of all nations, baptizing them in the name of the Father and of the Son and of the Holy Spirit, and teaching them to obey everything that I have commanded you' " (Matthew 28:18-20). Although the word "Trinity" is not used, its meaning is evident from Christ's words. Church practice and liturgical usage have confirmed the meaning.

tireless defender of the Council of Nicaea and of the Church's ancient biblical faith in the divinity of Christ and the mystery of the Trinity. Collusion between Arian bishops and emperors forced Athanasius from office five times, resulting in seventeen years in exile. At one point, he found support from the most admired saint of the times, St. Antony the Abbot, who agreed to leave his desert world for the first and only time to lend his presence and faith to the cause of the true faith. The old abbot awed the bishops, the people, and the political powers, causing a temporary truce in the theological battles of the age.

Athanasius spent the last seven years of his life back in office. Cardinal Newman praised him as "a principal instrument after the Apostles by which the sacred truths of Christianity have been conveyed and secured to the world."

So how do we make known the mystery of three Persons in one God, to which Athanasius devoted his life to defending? Many have grappled with ways to proclaim the mystery of the Trinity. St. Patrick told the Irish that the Trinity was like a shamrock. The three leaves on the one stem are like the three Persons in the one God. Others used the image of a candle flame. The red, white, and blue colors of the one fire stand for the three Persons in the one divine nature. Some employed the illustration of a tree with its roots, trunk, and fruit, differing in parts but united in the one tree. These down-home images of a shamrock, flame, and tree helped many people — but often a stirring hymn makes the point with a brilliant organ and trumpets, as with a thousand people we sing our faith in the Trinity:

> Holy, Holy, Holy! Lord God almighty!
> All thy works shall praise thy name in earth and sky
> and sea;

Holy, Holy, Holy! merciful and mighty,
God in three persons, blessed Trinity.

Incidentally, the use of song to stir hearts and minds was a lesson used by Arius. He composed anti-Trinity hymns for the shopkeepers, marching songs for the soldiers, and sea shanties for the sailors. St. Ambrose, a contemporary of St. Athanasius and bishop of Milan, responded by deliberately dramatizing his cathedral services with colorful liturgies and strong hymns, as well as his own pro-Trinity chants. In Ambrose's opinion, music not only soothed the savage breast, but it also helped correct false doctrine. Athanasius touched the mind with the wonder of three Persons in one God using the philosophy of person and substance. Ambrose appealed to the heart with his songs of praise of the Trinity. Together they defended the truth of the Trinity.

At the beginning of every Mass, we make the Sign of the Cross and declare that we enter into the liturgy "in the name of the Father, and of the Son, and of the Holy Spirit." At the end of Mass, we are blessed in the name of each Person of the Trinity, again making the Sign of the Cross as we are sent forth to witness our Trinitarian God in our everyday life. Most Catholics, when they enter their church, dip their hand in the holy water font and make the Sign of the Cross, invoking the Persons of the Trinity. This particular practice is meant to recall our baptism and is a way of renewing, in a general manner, our baptismal promises. Family meal prayers often invoke the Trinity. All blessings of religious articles or Church buildings involve the Sign of the Cross and the Trinitarian words.

Augustine and the Trinity

An expert on the teachings of the Church Fathers, Robert Louis Wilken writes that St. Augustine framed his masterpiece *On the Trinity* with the words from Psalm 105:3-4: "Let the hearts of those who seek the LORD, rejoice.... Seek his face always" (NIV). Augustine loved this quote and returned to it often. He concluded his treatise by adding the Latin word *ardenter* to the verse: "Seek his face always *with burning desire*." Wilken wondered what Augustine was seeking and why he asked his readers to seek with him. Augustine answered that he "wishes to enter into the presence of the Lord our God with all who read what I write."

Wilken comments further: "What Augustine is seeking is not a theological conception or an explanation as such, but the living God who is Father, Son and Holy Spirit, the Trinity that is God, the true and supreme and only God. What does this mean? The answer is not so obvious. 'Finding' means more than simply getting things straight or discovering the most appropriate analogy in human experience for the triune God. Our minds must be purified, and we must be made fit and capable for receiving what is sought. We can cleave to God and see the Holy Trinity only when we burn with love. There is no finding of God without a change in the seeker." [9]

Most liturgical prayers are directed to the Father, through the Son in the Holy Spirit. It requires our devotional attention to recall the meaning of these gestures and words, especially after many years of usage, since routine dulls the attention. Review of our call to reverence ignites our devotion and concentration.

For Reflection

1. What examples of fatherhood would help you appreciate the Fatherhood of God?
2. How does Jesus reveal God to you?
3. How real is the presence and action of the Holy Spirit in your life?
4. What images help you appreciate the mystery of the Holy Trinity? Why is it important to realize that all three Persons act each time a divine action is revealed to us?

Prayer

Batter my heart, three person'd God, for you
As yet but knock, breathe, shine, and seek to mend;
That I may rise and stand, o'erthrow me, and bend
Your force to break, blow, burn, and make me new....
Take me to you, imprison me, for I,
Except you enthrall me, never shall be free.

— JOHN DONNE, FROM HIS PRAYER TO THE HOLY TRINITY

CHAPTER SEVEN

THE HEAVENS DECLARE THE GLORY OF GOD

In the beginning God created the heavens and the earth. — GENESIS 1:1, RSV

Some scriptural commentaries and scientific criticisms blissfully take the sublime text that is the Creation story apart like a mechanic looking under the hood of the family car. But the text is not an engine; it is God's love song as he effortlessly unfolds light and darkness, sun and moon, oceans and fish, mountains and plains, trees and grain, lions and birds, and then moves another curtain aside and his divine masterpiece appears — man and woman.

Because we have heard the story so often, our minds submit unawares to a "film of familiarity" that hides the beauty and truth of what is actually there. The Creation story is so well known that our mental "cataracts" cease to be touched by the wonder and awe that the biblical words are meant to communicate. And yet the wonder and awe remain.

"The world did not come into being spontaneously, as some have imagined, but was brought about by God. Anyone who does not enjoy intimacy with God is unable to see the works of God."

— ST. BASIL OF CAESAREA, *HOMILY ON CREATION*

Three perennial questions arise about the Creation narrative. The answers come from our faith:

1. **Why did God create the world?** Love motivated God's creativity. Over and over the Creator says, "That's good." The will of God is a decision that proceeds from a love that always wills the good. The three Persons of the Trinity wanted to create the Garden of Eden and the beginning of a human race that would be the beneficiary of the divine love, goodness, and joy that could come from union with God. Creation is never an impersonal event; it is the outcome of divine wisdom. The psalmist got it exactly right when he sang, "O Lord, how manifold are your works! In wisdom you have made them all" (Psalm 104:24). That basic plan never disappeared, for when the human race fell into sin, the Son of God came to us and said: "God so loved the world that he gave his only Son, so that everyone who believes in him may not perish but may have eternal life" (John 3:16).

2. **How did God create the world?** The Lord God created the world out of nothing. When we build a house, we use existing materials such as wood, bricks, steel, glass, and tiles. Artists are a little closer to God's way of creating. Yet even Michelangelo needed a block of marble to produce the *Pietà*, although he liked to say with considerable modesty: "I see the figure inside the marble. All I do is let it out." God created the marble out of nothing. The sculptor makes a human figure out of that marble.

3. **How does God share his creativity with us?** God has given us the gift of imagination, art, and craft to

imitate his creativity and participate in the ongoing process of creation. The Holy Spirit inspires us and endows us with the gifts to participate in the highest form of creativity: the life of holiness that surrenders our souls to him, that we may be shaped into saints. Any time we share in God's authentic creativity, we extend divine goodness into the world.

4. **What do we mean by "God's providence"?** Let's say you had been living in a small house that was uncared for. No one had ever taught you how to clean the floor, wash the windows, repair the roof, get rid of the bugs, nurture the tiny grass plot in front, freshen the beds, polish the furniture, and fix the doors. Now someone gives you a nice, new big house. But the donor gives it to you and then disappears. You don't know how to take care of it, so within a year your new home begins to look like the little old house that was falling apart.

In a much deeper sense, our world is a remarkable cosmic house, and our souls and bodies are even more incredible creations. God understood that his creation always needed his abiding presence and care. He did not create Adam and Eve and then leave them orphans. "God's providence" means that he remains present to creation, to oversee our destiny and to maintain us and the universe in existence. God is present to the process to help make sure the "house" is in order. Even though we presently have more than six billion human beings on earth, our great cosmic home is in need of repair, not to mention the millions of hungry souls that have yet to know the oceanic love of God. Jesus taught that the beauty of the lilies of the field comes from God's attention to them: "Will

he not much more clothe you — you of little faith?"
(Matthew 6:30). We have the cosmic home. We have
human ingenuity. We also need faith in God's providential care. God expects us to cultivate the garden of
the world, and he is always ready to help us.

Easter is the rest of the Genesis story. Despite the efforts of Communism, in the old Christian cultures of Eastern Europe, Easter is the favorite feast. On that day, the
greeting and reply tell the tale: "Christ is risen!" — "He
is risen indeed!" The Easter Vigil and the fifty days of

Scientific Studies of the Origin of the World

"The question about the origins of the world and of man
has been the object of many scientific studies which
have splendidly enriched our knowledge of the age
and dimensions of the cosmos, the development of life-
forms and the appearance of man.... The great interest
accorded to these studies is strongly stimulated by a
question of another order, which goes beyond the proper
domain of the natural sciences. It is not only a question
of knowing when and how the universe arose physically,
or when man appeared, but rather of discovering the
meaning of such an origin: is the universe governed
by chance, blind fate, anonymous necessity, or by a
transcendent, intelligent and good Being called 'God'?
And if the world does come from God's wisdom and
goodness, why is there evil? Where does it come from?
Who is responsible for it? Is there any liberation from it?"

— CCC, 283-284

the Easter Season, in both East and West, are filled with creation imagery. The sacraments of the new creation — Baptism, Confirmation, and Eucharist — penetrate the liturgies of Easter time. Through the ministry of the Church, the Lord of history, the Risen Christ, is the herald of the new creation who strides about the earth baptizing, confirming, feeding his flock with his Body and Blood, and singing to them, "I will raise you up. I will raise you up on the last day."

The very first reading at the Easter Vigil is the Creation story from the first chapter of Genesis. This is not just a matter of looking back; it is the Church's way of proclaiming that our end, our goal, is in the beginning. The mystery of creation in the Genesis narrative contains a remarkable outcome — namely, that in the Son of God there will be a new creation where death is overcome and eternal life is made available now.

Our devotion to the Risen Christ affirms our faith that in death our lives are changed, not taken away, and that one day our bodies will rise again. This is the reason for the Catholic respect for the bodies of the dead. It is also why we have a special reverence for the relics of the saints. In the early Church, the buried bodies of the martyrs became shrines to which pilgrims came, a custom that continues today. The new creation embodied by the Risen Christ fulfills what the first creation was all about.

For Reflection

1. When you think of the term "create," what comes to your mind? What is the difference between the way humans create and the way God creates?

2. In the eighteenth century, the deists taught that God made the world but then left it to us to manage. Why do we disagree with them, and in what ways can we see God's providential care for the world?
3. In a culture where we do not like to think of death or the afterlife, how does our devotion to the relics of the saints help us appreciate the role of death in our lives?

———

Prayer

Almighty God, our creator and redeemer, by your power our Lord Jesus Christ conquered death and ascended to you in glory. May all who have gone before us in faith share in this victory and enjoy the vision of your glory forever in your heavenly kingdom. Amen.

— Adapted from the Opening Prayer for the
Third Mass for All Souls' Day

CHAPTER EIGHT

HOW TO BECOME AN IMAGE OF GOD

> *God created man in his own image … male and female he created them.* — GENESIS 1:27, RSV

Visualize the center of the ceiling of the Sistine Chapel. God rides on a cloud toward Adam. Dreamlike, Adam stretches out his arm and extends one finger to touch the hand of the Lord. In the fresco, the small empty space between God's hand and Adam's finger shows they do not touch. But most of the millions who have beheld the scene know that God's life-creating power is surging into Adam. There is nothing frail or lifeless about the bodies of God and Adam. The scene is an engaging way to illustrate the mystery of our creation.

Michelangelo (1475-1564) always loved God. His faith told him he must picture God the Creator with such magnificence that all who would see him would nod their heads and say, "Yes! That is God!" He had to imagine in human terms how God looked, felt, and poured out his divine power. He aimed at depicting a God the Father whom all could accept and adore.

Irving Stone's fictional account of the artist's struggle to produce an unforgettable vision of God creating Adam is captured in the following quote:

Since he [God] had created man in his own image, he had the face and body of a man. The first human whom God created, Adam, had surely been fashioned in his likeness. By setting forth Adam, the son, true creature of the Father: magnificent in body, noble in thought, tender in spirit, beautiful in face and limb, archetype of all that was finest in heaven and on earth, there would be reflected God, the Father. God, in clinging white robe which matched his virile white beard, had only to hold out his right arm to Adam, to reach one infinitesimal life-breath more, man and the world would begin.[10]

Michelangelo wanted us to understand that we are created in the image of God. But who do some in our culture say that we are?

Euro-American culture claims that I am what I do. I am my profession, my job, my talent. I am a singer, a pro-football player, a bishop, a movie star, a concert pianist, a garbage collector, a politician, a waitress, a teacher, a bookkeeper, a coal miner, a computer hacker, a journalist, a nun. That's what I do; that's who I am. I am my function in life. But the Lord says, "I have called you by name, you are mine…. You are precious in my sight…. See, I have inscribed you on the palms of my hands" (Isaiah 43:1, 4; 49:16).

Others in the culture swell up and proclaim I am what I have. I am my mega-house, my standing on the Fortune 500, my bank account, my investments. I am my closets filled with expensive clothes. I am my upscale cars. I am my ski vacations in St. Moritz, my trips to Paris, my cruises. I am my jewels and the gold in my bank's safe. I am what I own. But God says, "You fool! This very night your life is being demanded of you. And the things you have prepared, whose will they be?" (Luke 12:20).

A third group slyly smirks and says I am my sexual identity. I am a sexual subject always prowling for a sexual object. I am my porno sites on the computer. I am my skill in chasing women. I am my success in seducing men. I am my music arranged for arousal. I am sexually free from restraints. The only thing I want to control is birth. However, God says, "Therefore a man leaves his father and his mother and clings to his wife, and they become one flesh" (Genesis 2:24, RSV); and Jesus continued, "What therefore God has joined together, let no man put asunder" (Matthew 19:6, RSV).

So what does it mean to be made in the image and likeness of God? William Shakespeare's *Hamlet* gives us a good start: "What a piece of work is man! how noble in reason! how infinite in faculty! ... in action how like an angel! in apprehension how like a god!" For the playwright, to be human is to be able to think, to desire endlessly, to act like an angel, to know and understand "like a god." Man and woman are compared to beings beyond them, like an angel and a god.

The psalmist weighs in with equal admiration, praising God's majesty and marveling at what God did for us: "What is man that you are mindful of him...? Yet you have made him little less than the angels, and you have crowned him with glory and honor. You have given him dominion over the works of your hands; you have put all things under his feet" (Psalm 8:4, 5-6, RSV).

The human person is created in the image of God in the sense that he or she is capable of knowing and loving the Creator in freedom. The capacity for knowledge, love, and freedom are keys to being an image of God. Precisely because they are images of God, all human beings have the dignity of a person. A person is not a something but a someone, capable of self-knowledge. Such a person is able to enter into deep relationships with God and other persons. God has given humans the capacity of sharing in his divine life. Therefore, I am more than what I do. I am someone who can freely know and love God and other people. What I do is meant to help me fulfill that calling.

Therefore, I am more than what I have. Possessions are a means to an end, which is final union with God. If I am what I own, I am poor indeed. All we own we owe to

"I Learned to Love Human Love"

"As a young priest I learned to love human love. This has been one of the fundamental themes of my priesthood — my ministry in the pulpit, in the confessional, and also in my writing. If one loves human love, there naturally arises the need to commit oneself completely to the service of 'fair love,' because love is fair, it is beautiful.

"After all, young people are always searching for the beauty in love. They want their love to be beautiful. If they give in to weakness … they still desire a beautiful and pure love. This is as true of boys as it is of girls. Ultimately, they learn that only God can give them this love. As a result, they are willing to follow Christ, without caring about the sacrifices this may entail.

"As a young priest and pastor I came to this way of looking at young people and at youth, and this has remained constant all these years. It is an outlook which allows me to meet young people wherever I go."[11]

— POPE JOHN PAUL II

God, the giver of all good things. The goods of the earth are meant to be for the good of all.

Therefore, I am more than my sexual identity, a sexual subject exploiting a sexual object. True sexuality is a noble form of love and responsibility, of rights and duties, of a permanent covenant, like the commitment God has for us. Images of God possess God-like fidelity.

Which brings us to an essential question: How do I live as an image of God? Here are four ways to begin:

1. **Believe in your capacity to know God and the truth.** Our first way of practicing being images of God is to say to ourselves, "I believe there is truth and that I can know it." Jesus, who in his humanity was the perfect image of God, claimed that he knew the truth, that he *was* truth itself. The most popular enemy of faith is skepticism, and its first law is that we have no ability to know truth or God. Today's skeptics begin their campaign to undermine Catholic faith in God by arguing there is no truth — and if it did exist, we could not know it. Their position is self-contradictory. How can a skeptic who knows no truth propose as a truth that it doesn't exist?

2. **Do small things with great love.** God is love. The most powerful passion we experience is the longing to love and to be loved. To be an image of God is to love others as we love ourselves. Mother Teresa says, "In this life we cannot do great things. We can only do small things with great love." St. Teresa of Ávila recommends that we make constant acts of love for God, for "this sets our souls on fire."

3. **Be always aware you are a person, not a thing.** Respect yourself as a person of dignity. That's how God made you. At first, Adam only had animals for company. He felt lonely, and God said it is not good for a man to be alone. Adam needed human company. God created Eve and presented her to Adam, who received her with whoops of joy! "This at last … is flesh of my flesh" (Genesis 2:23).

4. **Form a communion with others and God.** The First Community is the Trinity. The love of the divine Persons for one another models what they expect from

Twenty-Five Hundred Images of God

During World War II, Irena Sendler (1910-2008), a social worker, served as a member of the Polish resistance to the Nazis. Secretly, she saved 2,500 Jewish babies from destruction in the Warsaw Ghetto, carrying them out in boxes and suitcases, and placing them with Polish families. When the Nazis discovered her, they took her to a forest, broke her arms and legs, and left her to die. Her friends saved her. Nominated for the Nobel Peace Prize as a hero, she replied: "I'm not a hero. I continue to have pangs of conscience that I did not do more."

From the Israeli people, she received the Yad Vashem Medal as one of the Righteous Among the Nations, an honor given to non-Jews who saved Jews from extermination during the Holocaust. She said, "Every child saved by my help is the justification of my life on earth. It is not a title to glory." In 2003, Pope John Paul II sent her a personal letter praising her wartime efforts in saving 2,500 images of God.

their six billion images on earth. Images of God are not lone rangers or lonely rangers. As John Donne puts it, "No man is an island, entire of itself.... Any man's death diminishes me, because I am involved in mankind, and therefore never send to know for whom the bell tolls; it tolls for thee."

For Reflection

1. How would you answer those who claim we have no ability to know the truth even if truth does exist?
2. In what ways do people mistreat human dignity? How can you counter this in your own life?
3. How often do you see the people around you as images of God?

Prayer

Dear Jesus, help me to spread Thy fragrance everywhere I go. Flood my soul with Thy spirit and love. Penetrate and possess my whole being so utterly that all my life may only be a radiance of Thine. Shine through me and be so in me that every soul I come in contact with may feel Thy presence in my soul. Let them look up and see no longer me but only Jesus. Stay with me and then I shall begin to shine as You shine, so to shine as to be a light to others.

— MOTHER TERESA, FROM THE VIDEO
EVERYONE, EVERYWHERE

CHAPTER NINE

PRIMAL SIN AND PROMISED SALVATION

> *Sin is present in human history. This reality of sin can be understood clearly only in the light of divine revelation and above all in the light of Christ the Savior of all. Where sin abounded, he made grace to abound all the more.* — COMPENDIUM, 73

God created Adam and Eve and placed them in the Garden of Eden. God told them to cultivate the garden and said they could eat the fruit of all the trees, except the tree of the knowledge of good and evil. The forbidden tree symbolized their human limits. Their desire for the infinite could not be satisfied by a finite means. God asked them for trust and obedience.

The tempter came to Eve and urged her to eat the forbidden food. She protested that she would die as a result. The tempter denied that this would happen. Instead, he said, she and her husband would become like God. Eve saw that the fruit was pleasing and desirable, and she ate it. She surrendered to the temptation, and then she gave some to Adam and he ate it as well.

For the first time, they felt shame and covered their private parts. They heard God's voice seeking them out and they hid in the bushes. They had declared their independence from God. They wanted to get away so that he could not find them. But God saw them, of course, and then asked: "Why are you hiding?" Adam replied, "I was afraid because I was naked."

Now we see some effects of the primal sin: Fear. Nakedness. Hiding. The blame game begins. The tempter blames God. Eve blames the tempter. Adam blames Eve. Personal responsibility is abdicated. Because of this first sin, Adam and Eve lost the garden. Childbirth would be painful. Farming would be backbreaking. They would suffer and die.

During their life in the garden, Adam and Eve enjoyed original holiness and justice. These spiritual gifts enabled them to master their inner life and bodily passions. The man and woman lived in harmony and peace. They possessed a positive attitude toward creation and related to God with love, trust, and obedience.

By their sin, they were deprived of original holiness and justice. They lost inner harmony and experienced their flesh warring against their spirit. Now they knew tensions, lust, and the drive to dominate. Fear colored their relationship with God. They needed to tame a hostile environment. Suffering and death entered history. Yet, even in this dark moment God promised a new creation, a redemption that would be greater than the first creation.

St. Augustine called the disobedience of Adam "original sin." Supporting Augustine, the Council of Trent taught that original sin is passed on by propagation, not imitation. We inherit it; we do not commit it.

This teaching affects the understanding of our moral and spiritual life. It responds to the nagging question, "Why is there something wrong with me?" We were born good but flawed, with an inclination to sin that traces back to Adam. Sin is a condition from which we need to be rescued by Christ's saving acts. "For just as by the one man's

"O Happy Fault!"

"Why did God not prevent the first man from sinning? St. Leo the Great responds, 'Christ's inexpressible grace gave us blessings better than those the demon's envy had taken away' (*Sermo* 73, 4: PL 54, 396). And St. Thomas Aquinas wrote, 'There is nothing to prevent human nature's being raised up to something greater, even after sin; God permits evil in order to draw forth some greater good. Thus St. Paul says, "Where sin increased, grace abounded all the more"; and the Exultet sings, "O happy fault, ... which gained for us so great a Redeemer" ' [*STh* III, 1, 3 *ad* 3; cf. Rom 5:20]."

— CCC, 412 (EMPHASIS IN ORIGINAL)

[Adam's] disobedience the many were made sinners, so by the one man's [Christ's] obedience the many will be made righteous.... Where sin increased, grace abounded all the more" (Romans 5:19, 20).

Through our baptism, we are delivered from original sin. No longer are we deprived of the possibility of holiness and justice and union with God. However, although the Sacrament of Baptism takes away the state of original sin, it does not remove all of its effects. Darkness still clouds our minds, our wills still falter in doing good, and our passions still remain rebellious. In other words, we still are inclined toward evil.

On the other hand, God endows us with an abundance of graces that purify us from evil tendencies, strengthen our moral resolve, and set us on the road to holiness. The sources of these graces include the sacraments, especially the Eucharist and Reconciliation, the gifts of the Holy Spirit, the power of prayer, the imitation of Christ, the inspiration of witnesses to Christ around us, and the intercession of Mary and the saints.

Armed with these sources of holiness, we set out on our spiritual and moral journey to God. Our special partner is Jesus, who walks with us, having lived in our humanity. He knows firsthand what we experience in everything, except sin. He can sympathize with our human struggles because he has lived on our side of creation. His every thought, word, and deed — his silences, words, actions, and all that happened in his passion, death, and resurrection — are now infinite fountains of life to slake our thirst and satisfy our hunger through the stages of spiritual growth we need to travel.

No temptation that seizes us need discourage us, for Jesus has been there, done that, and triumphed, not just for himself, but for us. No fall along the way should make us lose heart, for Christ's falls on the Way of the Cross glow with divine power to pick us up and move us forward.

Slippery Grace

A fourteenth-century mystic, Julian of Norwich, gently mocked our taste for reducing mystery to something physical or measurable. She pointed out that grace is slippery and not subject to confinements. It is fluid and floating. She pointed out that as the body is clad in cloth and the flesh is clothed in skin, and the bones in the flesh, and the heart in the torso, so are we, soul and body, enclosed in the goodness of God. All else wears away, but the goodness of God remains.

No failure dare stop us in our tracks when the cross was a victory over evil. No amount of rejection need strip us of our resolve to be saints when we can draw new life from the Christ who forgave all those who rejected him at Calvary and even excused them, *for they knew not what they did.*

Secularism seems more enamored with power of the mind than with love, whose influence does not appear to be important. Yet, what we think is less than what we know. What we know is less than what we love. Thoughts like these puzzle our pragmatic culture. St. Paul tells us that the only thing that will last after all is said or done is love. Paradise was lost by Adam and Eve, but a greater paradise has been given us by Christ.

For Reflection

1. Our first parents lost paradise through pride and disobedience and a failure to trust in God. How can we also lose the graces of salvation — our new creation?
2. Which parables of Christ motivate you to understand God's love and grace?
3. What is the difference between saying "I have experienced a failure" and "I am a failure"?

Prayer

Father in heaven, I turn to you in quest for the gift of love. From your revelation, I know that you and your Son and Spirit form a communion of love. Help me to trust in you and make love of you and others the primary goal of my life. Fill me with awe and reverence for the mystery of love. Help me to be overtaken by your grace that makes love possible in my life. Amen.

CHAPTER TEN

JESUS — OUR WAY TO GOD

> *"I am the way, and the truth, and the life. No one comes to the Father except through me."* — JOHN 14:6

Blessed Columba Marmion (1858-1923) wrote, "Christ is the Way, the only way to lead us to God, and without him we can do nothing. Our holiness has no other foundation than the same one which God has established, that is to say, union with Jesus Christ." Blessed Columba put Christ at the center of all his writings and teachings. His strong use of Scripture, especially the writings of St. Paul, was unique for his time, as were his perspectives of the Church Fathers. He united theology, Scripture, liturgy, and prayer into a single and forceful vision of how to relate to Christ, who in turn brings each person to his Father and the Spirit and the Church.

Born in 1858 in Dublin, Ireland, Joseph Marmion wanted to be a missionary to Australia — but after a visit to the Benedictine Abbey of Maredsous in Belgium, he felt a call to be a monk. His bishop persuaded him to wait five years and serve the pastoral needs of the diocese. Marmion's decision remained steady, and in 1886 the bishop permitted him to enter the abbey.

Taking the name Columba, he learned the ways of monastic discipline and community life, and he took solemn vows in 1891. He was appointed prior and theology professor at their house in Louvain and was elected abbot in 1909. He became well known as a retreat master and spiritual director. His inspiring conferences were collected in his popular books, including *Christ, the Life of the Soul*. He never deviated from his dynamic vision of union with God through Christ, who is the life of grace in our souls. Pope John Paul II beatified him on September 3, 2000.

The secret that Blessed Columba understood is that of divine adoption. What Jesus is by nature, we can receive

Center Your Heart on Christ

"The word of Christ is contained in the Gospels which, with the letters of St. Paul and St. John, are the most supernatural, because they are an inspired exposition of Christ's mysteries. The child of God therein finds the best title to divine adoption and the model to imitate. Look at our Lord and contemplate his actions; that is the most direct way of knowing God. To see him is to see his Father. He only is one with his Father. He only does what is pleasing to his Father. Each of his actions is the object of his Father's complacency, and we should delight in making it the object of our contemplation.

"That is why the words of Christ ought to abide in us so as to become in us principles of life. That is the reason too why it is useful for the soul that desires to live by prayer to read the Gospels constantly, and to follow the Church, our mother, when she represents to us the actions and recalls the words of Jesus in the course of the liturgical cycle. In making all the stages of the life of Christ, her Bridegroom and our Elder Brother, pass before our eyes, the Church supplies us with abundant food for prayer."[12]

— BLESSED COLUMBA MARMION

by the grace of adoption begun at Baptism and continued in the other sacraments, fellowship with the Church,
prayer, and witness.

At the beginning of history, just after the fall of Adam
and Eve, God promised the world a Savior. That Savior
turned out to be his beloved Son, Jesus Christ. Conceived
by the Holy Spirit and born of the Virgin Mary, Jesus fulfilled the Father's promise. Son of God and son of Mary,
Jesus would deliver us from the weight of sin and death.
"God so loved the world that he gave his only Son, so that
everyone who believes in him might not perish but may
have eternal life" (John 3:16).

We can appreciate the great gift of salvation only if
we recover the reality and meaning of the weight of sin.
On a practical level, we normally think of sin as disobey-
ing the Ten Commandments and other rules of the Bible
and the Church. This is true, of course, but it may not get to
the root of the matter. What does the First Commandment
say? "I am the LORD your God ... you shall have no other
gods before me" (see Exodus 20:2-3). God describes sin
in terms of a relationship. If you wonder about this, turn to
another text where God makes very clear what he means:
"You shall love the LORD your God with all your heart,
and with all your soul, and with all your might" (Deuteronomy 6:5). This is the greatest of all commandments.

God sets down the criterion of total love between
him and us. God's Son, Jesus, repeats this truth in the
same words. We need to love in order to have an identity.
The focus of our love determines how rich or poor will be
our identity. If our focus is sex, money, or power, these
"gods" will betray us and wreck our identity.

God has set the basic guideline for our relationship
with him. Negatively, he tells us: "Don't adore false gods,

the illusions you create for yourself." Positively, our Lord relays the same message: "My son, my daughter, give me your whole heart. Make me the highest priority in your life and forget the god-substitutes. Fold up the umbrella that prevents my sunlight from reaching you. Give up hiding from me and let me unfold the real self-identity you have always sought. Pay attention to the first of the Ten Commandments, and to the first and greatest commandment of Christ, and then all the others make sense."

Sin has been called a "sickness unto death," an illness of the soul that deadens it. What is the sickness? It is our fear of living in the sight of God. We are afraid of being utterly transparent, allowing all we are to be seen by God. Of course, God sees every part of us. But in our view of the relationship, we often attempt to conceal our souls from God. Like Adam and Eve, we still imagine we can hide in the bushes. We deliberately blur the relationship so that we can nurture our identity with something less than God. God sees us, but we refuse to see him. He is not, however, spying on us. Instead, with welcome in his eyes, he waits, with his arms outstretched to love us. Night and day Jesus stands patiently at the locked doors of our hearts. He knocks in the hope we will open the door.

One of the reasons for today's culture wars is the loss of a loving relationship with Christ. The disorder originates in hearts that have been dedicated to serving the self rather than serving Christ. In the Old Testament, we saw God creating the world as a tapestry of sun, moon, stars, mountains and valleys, animals and people, in a universal harmony. God said to his masterpiece, "That's good!" Sin entered the world when we decided to serve ourselves rather than God.

The Solid Rock

"My hope is built on nothing less
Than Jesus' blood and righteousness.
I dare not trust the sweetest frame,
But wholly lean on Jesus' name.

"On Christ the solid rock I stand,
All other ground is sinking sand;
All other ground is sinking sand.

"When darkness veils his lovely face,
I rest on his unchanging grace.
In every high and stormy gale,
My anchor holds within the veil.

"On Christ the solid rock I stand,
All other ground is sinking sand;
All other ground is sinking sand."

— EDWARD MOTE

Yet, even today, the Lord still pleads with us to come to him and receive his love. Jesus calls all of us to come to him. Like Uncle Sam in the poster for military recruits, Jesus basically says: "I want You! Not your things. You!" What will be our response?

For Reflection

1. What are some of the god-substitutes you may be using to deprive you of a soul-satisfying relationship with Christ?

2. How can you make Christ the center of your life and dedication?
3. In what ways does thinking of sin as a hiding from God change your idea of how to mend your relationship with God? How do rules and laws fit in with this approach?

———

Prayer

You alone may speak to me and I to you, as a lover speaks to a beloved and as a friend to friend. For this is my prayer and desire, that I may be wholly united to you, and withdraw my heart from all created things; that through Holy Communion and frequent offering of the Eucharist, I may come to delight in heavenly things more and more.[13]

— THOMAS À KEMPIS

CHAPTER ELEVEN

MIGHTY LORD AND HUMBLE SERVANT

> *" 'And when was it that we saw you sick or in prison and visited you?' And the king will answer them, 'Truly I tell you, just as you did it to one of the least of these who are members of my family, you did it to me.' "* — MATTHEW 25:39-40

One of our spiritual goals is to see Christ in others. Caryll Houselander (1901-1954), an English Catholic laywoman, whose books on the spiritual life attracted a wide audience, forcefully promoted that message. After a troubled childhood and some bouts of illness, she won a scholarship to art school, where she stopped being a practicing Catholic and sought help from a number of Protestant ministers, none of whom satisfied her searching. She fell in love with an international spy, but the romance did not last.

Gradually, Caryll realized she was running away from what she really wanted — a return to the Catholic Church. A religious experience that she called a vision occurred on a rainy night while she was on her way to a store, and it helped draw her home to the Church. She said that she saw a huge Russian icon: "Christ was lifted above the world on our drab street…. His arms reaching, as it seemed, from one end of the world to the other…. Christ himself, with his head bowed down by the crown of gold, brooding over the world."[14]

Once more a practicing Catholic, Caryll devoted herself to writing books on prayer and her favorite theme: how to see Christ in others. Her most popular book, *The Reed of God*, vividly portrayed the way Christ works through us to help others.

Jesuit Father Charles Healey reflected on Caryll's visions by relating them to her faith growth:

> After a few days the vision faded. Christ was hidden once again for her, and in the years ahead she would see Christ in others only through an act of faith. But if the vision had gone from her, the knowledge remained, and she was to find that at the least touch of the Holy Spirit it was to flower again and again. For she saw that the knowledge gained from all three "visions" was like "a tiny little seed sown in the mind, which will increase and flower only through years of prayer and study of the doctrine of the Church, which invariably endorsed them."[15]

Her faith in Christ's presence in others, along with her remarkable insights into human nature, marked Caryll Houselander as a spiritual guide until her death at age 53.

Before we can see Jesus in others, we need to be sure we know who this Jesus is in whom we believe. For our salvation, it is crucial that Jesus be divine. Man alone could not save us. Only God could do it. For our salvation, it is crucial that Jesus also be human, for the process of salvation includes the sanctification of all the aspects of our humanity. Jesus became like us in all things except sin so that our human nature could be healed.

The four Gospels tell us that Jesus is both human and divine. The birth stories in Matthew and Luke proclaim

Christic Is Everywhere

"I was in an underground train, a crowded train in which all sorts of people jostled together, sitting and strap-hanging — workers of every description going home at the end of the day. Quite suddenly I saw with my mind, but as vividly as a wonderful picture, Christ in them all. But I saw more than that; not only was Christ in every one of them, living in them, dying in them, rejoicing in them, sorrowing in them — but because he was in them, and because they were here, the whole world was here too, here in this underground train; not only the world as it was at that moment, not only all the people in all the countries of the world, but all those people who had lived in the past, and all those yet to come.

I came out into the street and walked for a long time in the crowds. It was the same here, on every side, in every passer-by, everywhere — Christ."[16]

— CARYLL HOUSELANDER

his humanity as conceived by the Spirit and born of the Virgin Mary. John's first chapter discloses Jesus' divine origin as the Eternal Word who becomes flesh. Matthew teaches us that Jesus preached about and established the kingdom of God, a kingdom of salvation, love, mercy, and justice. Mark emphasizes the role of the cross in Christ's mission and our call to a discipleship in which we lose the self, take up our cross, and follow Christ. Luke dwells on the human face of Jesus, his compassion for the poor, the dignity of women, and the need to seek the lost sheep, the lost coin, the lost son and daughter.

In contrast, John lifts us to the heavenly realms to perceive the divine face of Jesus, whose ministry reveals his "glory" — that is, his divinity. God becomes human so that we might participate in divine life. Of course, all of the Gospels have the accounts of his passion, death, and resurrection, the ultimate cause of our salvation. Beyond the Gospels, the answers to the question "Who is Jesus?" flow like a river from the prophetic pages of the Old Testament and the powerful pen of St. Paul and other biblical writers. The wisdom of the teaching office of our Church (the Magisterium) throughout history has deepened the meaning of all these insights for our inspiration, prayer, and capacity for spiritual and moral growth.

How do we, then, practice seeing the Jesus we know in others around us?

Taking care of the needs of others is a stepping stone to seeing Christ in other people; it is the way to practice noticing Jesus in them. The twenty-fifth chapter of Matthew relates Christ's vision of the Last Judgment. The sheep — those who served Christ through taking care of the hungry, the naked, the imprisoned, the thirsty, the strangers, the sick, and others in need — will inherit the kingdom of heaven. The goats — those who ignored the face of Christ in the hungry, the naked, the imprisoned, the thirsty, the strangers, the sick, and others in need — will be sent to the eternal fire prepared for the devil and his angels.

St. Paul helps us understand by talking about all of us belonging to the Body of Christ: "For in the one Spirit we were all baptized into one body…. Now you are the body of Christ and individually members of it" (1 Corinthians 12:13, 27).

Jesus used another image, calling himself the vine and saying that we are the branches (John 15:5). Just as Christ's life flows through us as members of his Body, so his life pours into us as a vine nourishes its branches. The body and vine imagery reveal how intimate Christ's closeness is to us.

It requires faith to believe that you are part of Christ's Body or a branch on his vine. It is unlikely you will see Jesus in others without an active faith and prayer life that opens your eyes to see what Christ has planned for you. How did Mother Teresa dedicate herself to picking up destitute dying men and women in the gutters of Calcutta? Was it easy for her? Not really, at least not at first. It is said that when she began to treat lepers she became sick to her stomach and had to back away. But she asked Christ to show his presence in those unfortunate people. Christ said yes to her prayer, and in time she was able to not only wash and nurse the bodies of dying lepers, but she could also kiss them. And as we now know from her diaries released after her death, she did this for years during which she did not feel the presence of God.

For Reflection

1. How have you learned to see and serve Christ in others?
2. Why is it important to have a sound doctrinal understanding of the full identity of Jesus Christ, Son of God and son of Mary?
3. Faith, like a muscle in your body, grows stronger only with use. What are some ways to develop a stronger faith?

Prayer

Christ be with me, Christ within me,
Christ behind me, Christ before me,
Christ beside me, Christ to win me,
Christ to comfort and restore me.
Christ beneath me, Christ above me,
Christ in quiet, Christ in danger,
Christ in hearts of all that love me,
Christ in mouth of friend and stranger.

— FROM THE BREASTPLATE OF ST. PATRICK

CHAPTER TWELVE

SAVED BY HIS CROSS, RENEWED BY HIS RESURRECTION

> *The message about the cross is foolishness to those who are perishing, but to us who are being saved it is the power of God.* — 1 CORINTHIANS 1:18

In looking at the history of Christian devotion, we cannot escape the fact that devotion to the cross is a dominant theme. The poor, the sick, the oppressed, and the crushed find comfort in the Passion of Christ. The "man of sorrows" means a great deal to those dissolved in pain. The Crucified speaks to them when no one else seems to help.

Even today, the cross has power to move us.

During his second pastoral visit to the United States, Pope John Paul II went to Columbia, South Carolina, to meet with leaders of the Protestant and Orthodox faiths. After a private meeting, a prayer service was held in the University of South Carolina football stadium.

Sixty thousand people, mostly Protestants, crowded the stands, in a state that housed a small percentage of Catholics. The ceremony began with a procession of the many different religious leaders wearing their distinctive garb. As they paraded by, it was easy to see a colorful cameo of the last thousand years of Church history delineated by the various robes, from the Greek Orthodox to the Lutherans to the Baptists and many more.

An advocacy group protested the mounting of a cross on state university property, but agreed that the cross could be brought in when the pope actually arrived for the service. At a signal from the organ and orchestra, the assembly arose and began to sing the hymn "When I Survey the Wondrous Cross." The stately melody accompanied the appearance of five young men at the north side of an end zone, carrying a huge cross horizontally on their shoulders. On the south side came five young women bearing a large tapestry of the Lamb of God, slain and risen. Both groups processed to the other end zone where John Paul II stood to meet them. As they arrived before him, the congregation sang the last stanza: "Were the whole realm of nature mine, that were a present far too small; love so amazing, so divine, demands my soul, my life, my all." The young people then planted the wooden cross and the tapestry of the Risen Lord into university ground. The throng of believers praised God with hymns and prayers that honored the saving death and resurrection of the Son of God.

We love Easter, but we need the shadows of Good Friday to see the full possibilities of the Paschal Mystery. Consider this analogy: The most distant object we can see in the bright light of day is the sun, but in the darkness of night we can see the stars, which are millions of miles farther away. This is something to keep in mind when life plunges us into a bad patch that depresses us and robs us of confidence about the future.

Before he died, Jesus said: "When I am lifted up from the earth, [I] will draw all people to myself" (John 12:32). He had also said that the greatest form of love

The Suffering God

The Lutheran minister Dietrich Bonhoeffer (1906-1945)
expressed his belief in the power of the cross a few
days before his death on April 9, 1945, in Flossenbürg
concentration camp:

> God lets himself be pushed out of the world on to
> the cross. He is weak and powerless in the world,
> and that is precisely the way, the only way, in
> which he is with us and helps us. Matt. 8.17 [which
> quotes Isaiah 53:4: "He has borne our infirmities
> and carried our diseases"] makes it quite clear that
> Christ helps us, not by virtue of his omnipotence, but
> by virtue of his weakness and suffering.... Only the
> suffering God can help.[17]

was to die to save the beloved. In this sense, the cross is
the greatest sign of God's love. It is the heart of our faith.
Some Christians prefer to have a cross without the figure
of the Crucified. They argue that Christ is now risen. But
even the Risen Jesus retained the scars of the Passion. The
wisdom of the Church tells us that it is too easy to forget
the price of salvation. We need a picture of what Jesus
determined to do and what is expected of us. No pain, no
gain. No cross, no Easter.

Through his death, Jesus saved us from sin and the
finality of death. By his resurrection, he gained us a share
in his divine life and the promise of our own resurrection.
His dying and rising form a single act of salvation, for
both events were essential for saving us.

After his resurrection, he appeared at least five times. How do these appearances help us grasp the meaning of Easter?

1. **The appearance to Mary Magdalene.** All of the Gospels report that Mary Magdalene was among the first to see the Risen Lord. Jesus chose her because she loved him so much both in life and death. Of all his followers, she had the best capacity to accept the truth of his resurrection. Jesus picked her to be the first to announce the good news to the apostles. She now says to us, "Don't make the Resurrection a mind game. Love Christ with all your heart, and then your intelligence will be able to believe in this great and generous mystery of Christ. Believe, that you may understand."

2. **The appearance to the apostles on Easter night.** Jesus blessed his followers with three gifts: the gift of the Holy Spirit, the power to forgive sins, and the revelation of his glorified body, now not bound by time or space or decay. He found them full of fear, so he framed his gifts with his creative and powerful word, "Shalom — Peace." He reached into each of their souls and filled them with peace, order, purpose, and courage. The Risen Jesus does the same for us today. He gives us the Holy Spirit, the Sacrament of Reconciliation, the promise we will rise again with him, and lastly, the peace that surpasses all understanding.

3. **The appearance to two disciples.** Jesus met two disciples on the road to Emmaus. During this seven-

mile walk, he gave them a remarkable Bible lesson. "Then beginning with Moses and all the prophets, he interpreted to them the things about himself in all the scriptures" (Luke 24:27). He taught them the need for his suffering and death, himself as the unifying principle of interpreting Scripture. At the Emmaus meal, he took bread, blessed it, broke it, gave it to them, and then vanished. They recognized him in the "breaking of the bread," a name for Eucharist. This rich passage shows us the link between the cross, the Bible, the Eucharist, and the Risen Christ.

4. **The appearance at the lakeside.** Here Jesus completed his call to Peter to lead the Church. Peter's three denials required three acts of love to which Jesus replied that he should "feed my lambs," "tend my sheep," and "feed my sheep." Jesus had already made him the Rock (leader) of the Church. Now he made Peter the loving Shepherd and Pastor. Today the Risen Jesus assures us we are not leaderless; we have his vicar, who serves us as unifying shepherd.

5. **The appearance on the mountain.** This is the scene of the Great Commission. He gave the apostles three challenges: "Go therefore and [1] make disciples of all nations, [2] baptizing them in the name of the Father and of the Son and of the Holy Spirit, and [3] teaching them to obey everything that I have commanded you" (Matthew 28:19-20). Our living Easter Lord also commissions us to evangelize the world by making disciples, leading them to the sacraments, and urging them to witness him and his teachings in our families, schools, parishes, and society.

These five appearances of our Risen Lord still occur today. We still need the love of Mary Magdalene, the gifts of peace and the Holy Spirit, the lessons of Emmaus, the pastoral spirit of St. Peter, and the evangelizing courage first announced just before Christ's ascension.

For Reflection

1. How do you take up your cross and follow Jesus daily?
2. Which lessons from the Easter appearances of Christ have you incorporated into your life?
3. What are some ways to encourage the new evangelization in our parishes?

Prayer

On the third day, he rose again, glorious in majesty
    to reign;
O let us swell the joyful strain. Alleluia!

— FROM THE HYMN *THE STRIFE IS O'ER*

CHAPTER THIRTEEN

"BREATHE ON ME, HOLY SPIRIT"

> *We have received not the spirit of the world, but the Spirit that is from God, so that we may understand the gifts bestowed on us by God ... for the Spirit searches everything, even the depths of God.* — 1 CORINTHIANS 2:12; 2:10

St. Basil of Caesarea (330-379) wrote, "As the Father is seen in the Son, so the Son is seen in the Spirit. To worship the Spirit, then, is to have our minds open to the light, as we may learn from our Lord's words to the Samaritan woman. He told her that one must worship in Spirit and truth, and clearly by the truth he meant himself."

This saintly advocate of the Holy Spirit was born in Asia Minor to a family of saints that included his grandmother, parents, and oldest sister. Two other family members, in addition to Basil, became bishops. It was certainly fitting that, being nurtured in a household where so much holiness prevailed, Basil would write a famous treatise on the Holy Spirit. Besides being singularly blessed by the Spirit, he received an excellent education in schools at Caesarea, Constantinople, and Athens.

After his baptism in 358, Basil became a monk and visited many of the monasteries of the East. Eventually, he founded his own monastery and wrote a rule for monks that contained practical legislation for monasteries and another guidebook filled with prayerful paths to holiness. These works earned him the title "Legislator for Eastern Monasticism." He was later named bishop of Caesarea, where he defended the faith against the Arians. With his friend St. Gregory Nazianzen, he laid the foundation for the decision of the First Council of Constantinople to affirm the Church's ancient faith in the divinity of the Holy Spirit.

St. Gregory later wrote:

> The Old Testament proclaimed the Father clearly, but the Son more obscurely. The New Testament revealed the Son and gave us a glimpse of the divinity of the Spirit. Now the Spirit dwells among us and grants us a clearer vision of himself. It was not prudent, when the divinity of the Father had not yet been confessed, to proclaim the Son openly and, when the divinity of the Son was not yet admitted, to add the Holy Spirit as an extra burden, to speak somewhat daringly…. By advancing and progressing "from glory to glory," the light of the Trinity will shine in ever more brilliant rays."[18]

This "daring" statement of Gregory illustrates the divine teaching method that spreads out the revelation of the mystery of the Trinity over hundreds of years to give the minds of believers time to assimilate this grand truth. Though the full reality of the Spirit did not become clear until after Christ's ascension into heaven, it was hinted at many times throughout the entire history of salvation. In the first lines of the Creation story, God's "mighty breath" (the Spirit) swept over the chaos and introduced order and harmony. Later, God's choice of various leaders for his people was often accompanied by an infusion of the Spirit-inspired ecstasy. This was especially true of the selection of prophets, a fact recalled in the Nicene Creed: "We believe in the Holy Spirit, the Lord, the giver of life…. He has spoken through the prophets."

In the New Testament, while St. Paul and St. John often refer to the Spirit, St. Luke's Gospel and Acts con-

Knowing the Holy Spirit

"The Church, a communion living in the faith of the apostles which she transmits, is the place where we know the Holy Spirit:

— in the Scriptures he inspired;

— in the Tradition, to which the Church Fathers are always timely witnesses;

— in the Church's Magisterium [Teaching Office], which he assists;

— in the sacramental liturgy, through its words and symbols, in which the Holy Spirit puts us into communion with Christ;

— in prayer, wherein he intercedes for us;

— in the charisms and ministries by which the Church is built up;

— in the signs of apostolic and missionary life;

— in the witness of saints through whom he manifests his holiness and continues the work of salvation."

— CCC, 688

tain the most extensive and vivid accounts of the Spirit's presence and action in salvation history. In Luke's infancy narrative, the Spirit is busy inspiring Zachary, Elizabeth, and Mary and Joseph to obey the call of God and gain insight into the Lord's purposes. Later, when Jesus gives his first sermon in the Nazareth synagogue, Luke recounts Jesus' quoting from Isaiah, "The Spirit of the Lord is upon me," before applying the text to his mission.

But it is, of course, in the Acts of the Apostles that the revelation of the Spirit is most powerful. From the key scene of the "Descent of the Holy Spirit upon the Apostles," the dramatic influence of the Spirit glows more brightly on every page. The characters of Peter and Paul and other figures exhibit amazing courage as a result of the Spirit. When you think about the apostles — who witnessed Jesus control storms, walk on water, cure lepers, and raise Lazarus from the dead, as well as give mesmerizing sermons — and see that they did not really understand what he was saying and doing until after the descent of the Spirit, you begin to appreciate the Spirit's power. Even after Jesus' resurrection from the dead and forty more days of incredible appearances and spiritual formation, they were still frightened and unfocused. Their transformation had not yet taken place.

Then came the gift of the Holy Spirit at Pentecost. The fire of the Spirit touched them, penetrated their souls, and set them aflame with God-given courage, which in turn affected all the other virtues. There are those who say that courage is one of the best proofs for the existence of God's presence. Over and over again, the main characters in Acts display boldness and courage. Luke attributes this to the power of the Holy Spirit at work in their lives.

The first believers demonstrated resounding conviction in their preaching and a stirring bravery in the face of dangers and death.

One of the major signs of the Spirit's presence was the gift of healing. This was truly the "Good News" Gospel as foretold by Isaiah (35:5-6) for the messianic age. From Pentecost onward, the Book of Acts reports healings as almost commonplace. In the final chapter, while Paul is resting at Malta before finally sailing to Rome, he cures the father of the local island chief and proceeds to heal others who come to him.

One of the noticeable ministries inspired by the Holy Spirit was the disciples' powerful, evangelizing sermons. Discourses, sermons, addresses, and exhortations abound. The main thing to remember about these sermons is their evangelical character. They were aimed at changing the minds, hearts, and lives of their listeners. The Jesus the disciples preached was the long-awaited Savior predicted by the Old Testament. Those who proclaimed the Good News provided information, but they went beyond facts. They sought to convert the listeners and used arguments to convince them. But they were quick to agree that only the transforming power of the Holy Spirit can produce life-changing experiences. Conversion is always a miracle of grace. This was self-evident, for as soon as the disciples opened their mouths, they felt the power of the Holy Spirit surge through their voices and words. The "proof of the pudding" was in the "eating," in the sense that the disciples' preaching ministry converted thousands all over the Roman Empire to the Church, the sacraments, and the Christian way of life.

Babel and Pentecost

The artists of the Middle Ages loved to contrast the Tower of Babel with the "tower" of the Upper Room. Babel symbolized the fundamental divisions of people caused by selfishness and sin. Pentecost stood for the confident promise that such division was not a tragic necessity. The babbling and squabbling mob of Babel compared poorly with the peaceful and heartening unity of the Pentecost assembly. The first was a mob. The second was a community. A people without God lost the ability to communicate. A people suffused with the Spirit spoke heart to heart.

The brief and shining hour of Pentecost remains to charm and encourage us to this day. Our Church is another Upper Room. Like the 120 believers who waited with hearts open to the Spirit, we assemble to sing and pray.

Without God, we tend to build Babels of strife. At our Eucharist, the Holy Spirit builds Upper Rooms of community and love.

For Reflection

1. How did your confirmation and other experiences show you the influence of the Holy Spirit in your life?
2. Why do many people testify that the Holy Spirit makes them feel the presence of God?
3. Why should you invoke the Holy Spirit's graces when you go to Mass and confession, as well as when you have tough decisions to make?

Prayer

For the Seven Gifts of the Holy Spirit

Come, Holy Spirit, with the gift of WISDOM. Direct my
every thought, word, and deed to the greater honor
and glory of the Trinity.

Come, Holy Spirit, with the gift of KNOWLEDGE and love
of Jesus and Mary.

Come, Holy Spirit, with the gift of UNDERSTANDING, that I
may know myself and that I may know you more
deeply.

Come, Holy Spirit, that, with the gift of COURAGE, I may
serve you with a cheerful heart.

Come, Holy Spirit, with the gift of COUNSEL. Shape my
conscience according to the guidance of your holy law.

Come, Holy Spirit, with the gift of PIETY, that I may
always do the will of God.

Come, Holy Spirit, with the gift of FEAR OF THE LORD, that
I may fear to sin or ever be separated from the love
of Christ.

Amen.

CHAPTER FOURTEEN

THE CHURCH, MY MOTHER AND TEACHER

> *Christ loved the church and gave himself up for her, in order to make her holy by cleansing her with the washing of water by the word, so as to present the church to himself in splendor, without a spot or wrinkle or anything of the kind — yes, so that she may be holy and without blemish. —* EPHESIANS 5:25-27

Pope Adrian VI (1459-1523), a Dutchman, was the last non-Italian to be pope until the papacy of John Paul II. His brief reign of twenty months was buffeted by the pressures of the Reformation, the threat of a Muslim invasion of Europe, and excessive political rivalries. He was a man of good intentions but constrained by a brief tenure that limited his efforts at reform.

A legend about Adrian captures his many predicaments but also highlights his basic wisdom. According to the story, he commissioned a Renaissance painter to do a picture of the Church in a storm at sea, somewhat like Peter's boat in the Gospel scene. When the painting was finished, Pope Adrian and his cardinals came to view it.

They saw a huge ship resting peacefully on a sea as tranquil as a sheet of glass. The sails were still. The pope and his cardinals were piously kneeling in prayer on the main deck. The Catholic laity were safe and secure in their staterooms staring out at the world through the portholes. Beyond this quiet scene, at each end of the painting, were angry waves, bolts of lightning, and threatening clouds. Tossed and battered in this chaos were the Protestants, Muslims, and other enemies of the Church.

Disappointed and frowning, Pope Adrian said: "No, this is not Christ's Church. This is not Peter's boat." Then making a fist he hit the ends of the painting with his papal ring. "Christ commissioned us to be saved by helping these people to hear and accept the Gospel, not by gloating over their errors but by purifying ourselves in the sight of God and witnessing the saving power, love, and faith that Jesus expected of his apostles. To us he says as he did to Peter, 'O you of little faith. Why did you doubt me?'" Striking the painting again, Adrian said: "We need to be saved with these and these and these."

Adrian's dream is echoed in our day: "The Church in this world is the sacrament of salvation, the sign and the instrument of the communion of God and men" (CCC, 780).

"By virtue of the divine power received from her Founder, the Church is an institution that endures; but even more than an institution, she is a life that is passed on. She sets the seal of unity on all the children of God whom she gathers together."[19]

— HENRI DE LUBAC, S.J.

While we are thinking of pictures, see your parish church in your mind's eye. Next, picture your local cathedral. Finally, bring to mind St. Peter's Basilica in Rome.

Practically speaking, your parish church is "Church" for you. Your cathedral widens your vision of the Church to the local diocese. St. Peter's reminds you of the universality of the Church. Catholicism is a global Church, a diocesan Church, and a parish Church all at the same time.

Obviously, the Church is more than a building; it is a community of people who share the same faith and gather for worship mostly on Sundays, but also on weekdays, as well as for baptisms, weddings, and funerals. The central expression of Church is the celebration of the Eucharist and the other sacraments. The primary bonding experience of what happens in the parish, the diocese, and the Vatican is the Eucharist. The Body of Christ in this sacrament binds and builds up the Body of Christ, which is the assembly of all of the Church's members under the ministerial leadership of the pope, the bishop, and the local pastor.

Jesus in the Holy Eucharist gathers the global Church in his reach so that our Church (as we pray in the Creed) is one, holy, catholic, and apostolic. The Church is one, but she needs to seek unity with all Christian communities that are separated from it. The Church is holy, but every member must grow in holiness and lay aside sinfulness. The Church is universal, yet there are huge areas where the Church's membership is sparse, such as in most Muslim countries, China, and India. The Church is apostolic in a double sense: its faith is that of the apostles, whose successors, the popes and bishops, seek to maintain; in another sense, the apostolates, missions, and evangelizing efforts of the Church flow from this characteristic. Yet here again the Church is challenged to grow vocations to the priesthood and religious life, and to bridge the gap between the Gospel and the cultures.

One way of looking at the Church is with Vatican II's document on the Church (*Lumen Gentium*, 1964), which describes it as a mystery, a people and a structure.

The Church is, first, a mystery because it originates from God and therefore is neither a human invention nor a result of the consent of the governed. In this view, God the Father planned the Church; God the Son, Jesus Christ, instituted the Church; and the Holy Spirit revealed the Church at Pentecost. The Persons of the Trinity accomplished this through the patriarchs, prophets, kings, and wisdom speakers of the first covenant, and by Jesus and his apostles and other followers in the new covenant.

Second, the Church is the People of God in the sense that God called them into existence and formed them as his people. This happens first at Sinai, where God concluded a covenant with Israel as he said to them: "You have seen what I did to the Egyptians, and how I bore you on eagles' wings and brought you to myself. Now therefore, if you obey my voice and keep my covenant, you shall be my treasured possession out of all the peoples. Indeed, the whole earth is mine, but you shall be for me a priestly kingdom and a holy nation" (Exodus 19:3-6).

Jesus fulfilled what the Father began by instituting a new People of God — the Church. His Father created the first People from the twelve tribes of Israel. Jesus created the new People from the twelve apostles, led by Peter, the seventy-two disciples, and the women who ministered to Jesus. By his preaching of and witnessing to the kingdom of God, by his miracles, and by his death and resurrection, Jesus formed a new priestly, prophetic, and royal people. At the Last Supper, he instituted the Eucharist and the ministerial priesthood, which were essential elements of the Church in which God's people would participate and receive their Christian identity and call to mission.

Third, the Holy Spirit revealed the Church at Pentecost. The Spirit sustains the growth and existence of the Church in favorable and unfavorable times. The Spirit is present at every Eucharist to change the bread and wine into the Body and Blood of Christ through the service of the ordained priest. The Holy Spirit hovers over every Liturgy of the Word, ready to help the readers proclaim it with faith and to assist the homilists to break open the Word so that God's deep message is heard and functions as a life-changing event. The Holy Spirit broods over the Church to help her become a mother and teacher to all her members. The Spirit is the source of unity and love in a Church that has a structure of authority in the popes and bishops and those who collaborate with them. The hierarchy of the Church serves as a source of order, stability, continuity, trustworthy teaching, and sacramental life. At

The Mission of the Church Is Our Mission

"The Christian faithful are those who, inasmuch as they have been incorporated in Christ through Baptism, have been constituted as the people of God; for this reason, since they have become sharers in Christ's priestly, prophetic and royal office in their own manner, they are called to exercise the mission which God has entrusted to the Church. There exists a true equality among them in their dignity as children of God."

— *COMPENDIUM, 177*

the same time, the lay faithful bring Christ to the world and the public order.

This brief outline of the essential teachings about the Church cannot ignore the relationship between our faith and its practical application. Love in the abstract may attract passing interest. But love demonstrated in care for people's spiritual, intellectual, physical, and emotional needs arouses a passion for service that is intrinsically connected to religious devotion.

Ever the practical pastor, St. James writes plainly about this. When he uses the term "faith," he links it to the word "devotion":

> What good is it, my brothers and sisters, if you say you have faith but do not have works? Can faith save you? If a brother or sister is naked and lacks daily food, and one of you says to them, "Go in peace; keep warm and eat your fill," and yet you do not supply their bodily needs, what is the good of that? So faith by itself, if it has no works, is dead. (James 2:14-17)

In reality, the devotional Church is one of the largest charitable agencies in our country. Indigent care at our hospitals, schools for the poor, support for missions in developing countries, nursing homes, food pantries for the hungry, homes for the homeless, care for pregnant teens, and language classes for immigrants (as well as instructions on how to bank, find jobs, and negotiate their way in a strange society) are all part of the Church's ministry. In the great tradition of Scripture, we are still helping the widows, orphans, and strangers. Devotion without care for those in need hints of selfish interest. Devotion that eagerly serves the poor is true devotion, which is self-giving sacrifice.

___

For Reflection

1. Why is it important to see the Church as mystery, people, and structure?
2. How can you relate to the Church as one, holy, catholic, and apostolic?
3. What do you find yourself expecting of your pastor, bishop, and pope?

___

Prayer

Heavenly Father,
look upon our community of faith
which is the Church of your Son, Jesus Christ.
Help us to witness to his love
by loving all our fellow creatures without exception.
Under the leadership
of the Holy Father and the bishops
keep us faithful to Christ's mission
of calling all men and women
to your service so that there may be
"one fold and one shepherd."
We ask this through Christ our Lord.
Amen.[20]

CHAPTER FIFTEEN

DO WHATEVER JESUS TELLS YOU

> *Mary in effect shows us the "Way" who is her Son, the one and only Mediator. — COMPENDIUM, 562*

Mary exemplifies the praying Church. While the apostles were engaged in active ministry converting people to Christ and establishing Christian communities, Mary supported them with her prayers. The Novgorod School of icon painting, which flourished from the twelfth century through the sixteenth century, created an icon of Christ's ascension, which portrays this truth of Church life. Jesus is at the top, carried by angels into glory. Mary stands on earth, still and silent, with her hands extended in prayer. Two angels clothed in white form a protective wall that separates her from the activity in the rest of the icon. Beyond the angels are the apostles — full of movement, hands waving, feet moving, bodies arched in activity — men on the move to go forth and preach the Gospel. They represent the evangelizing Church, missionaries bringing Christ to the world. Mary, on the other hand, stands firmly in the center of the ecclesial community. From her rooted presence flows the prayer and stability the Church needs for fidelity to the mission of salvation. Her link with Jesus is fundamental. The icon is an ideal picture of the relationship between contemplation and action. After Pentecost, that relationship becomes Mary's gift to us.

> "If we ponder her life with St. John in their mountain home overlooking the city of Ephesus, we can see her engaged in her ministry of contemplative prayer while the mystical John wrote the most mystical of Gospels. It is not too far to imagine Mary's prayer also directed to the missionary work of St. Paul during his two years in Ephesus. It takes no stretch of faith-filled imagination to perceive the contemplative Mary standing in the midst of our global Church interceding for us so that we always do what Jesus asks of us."[21]
>
> — FATHER ALFRED MCBRIDE, O.PRAEM.

All of the blessings that God bestowed on Mary are directed to her relationship with Jesus, which in turn benefit you and me, the Church, and the world. The Rosary priest, Father Patrick Peyton, tells us that "Mary will be as good to you as you want her to be. It all depends on God's grace and your faith." This is the context of our meditation on five of the many blessings of Mary.

1. Mary Is Full of Grace

Mary heard about this privilege from the angel Gabriel at the Annunciation. God planned that she would be free from original sin from the moment of her conception in the womb of her mother, St. Anne. In addition, Mary would be free from all actual sin throughout her life. She is the sinless daughter of God. The Eastern Church calls her *Panagia* — the All-Holy One. In the passing of centuries, as the Church meditated on this remarkable blessing of Mary, the community of faith began speaking of her

Immaculate Conception. God planned that the mother of Jesus would receive the gift of Christ's redemption from the first moment of her existence.

2. Mary Is the Mother of God

All of Mary's privileges and greatness flow from her being the Mother of God. Her surrender to God's will at the Annunciation led to all her future gifts and blessings.

In the fifth century, the patriarch of Constantinople preached that Mary was mother only of the human Christ. The divine Son then joined the human child. A council of the Church was held at Ephesus in 431, at which the bishops affirmed the teaching of Scripture and the continuous faith of the Church that Mary was Mother of God from the beginning, for her child was always human *and* divine. Hence, she is called the *Theotokos* — the God-bearer. When we need a spiritual mother, we can and should turn to Mary. Resolve to stay near Mary every day as often as you can. She is the most loving and trustworthy of mothers.

3. Jesus Names Mary "Woman"

At the marriage feast of Cana, Mary tells Jesus that the newlyweds have no wine. Jesus calls his mother "Woman" and says this is not his "hour" to begin manifesting his glory. Mary simply tells the steward, "Do what Jesus tells you." Because of Mary's intercession, Jesus changes jars of water into wine and reveals his glory (divinity). In calling her "Woman," he elevates her role beyond biological motherhood to participate somehow in his saving work. At Calvary, he again calls her "Woman" when he entrusts John to her spiritual care, and by extension the future Church. As we struggle to live up to the demands of salvation that we receive in Baptism and the other sacraments, we need to benefit from Mary's powerful intercession on our behalf as we try to "do what Jesus tells us."

4. Mary Is the Mother of the Church

At the Second Vatican Council, Pope Paul VI announced a new title for Mary as "Mother of the Church." This brings Mary's maternal care closer to us. At Christmas, we behold her hovering over her little baby Jesus. At Pentecost, we see her seated in the center of the apostles and the 120 believers gathered to receive the Holy Spirit. Now Mary presides over the public birth of the Church. She once held the little body of Christ in her arms. Now she holds the ecclesial Body of Christ in her heart. Her energizing contemplative prayer radiated into the souls awaiting the Spirit for nine days of prayer. Other than Jesus, Mary is the closest key to God that has ever existed in the human race. The modern tendency is to treat the Church as simply a political institution filled with warts. Mary will have none of that cynicism. Just as she jealously protected her Son from crib to cross, she now pushes us to respect and reverence our gift of the Church, which is the Mystical Body.

5. Mary Is Assumed Into Heaven

When Mary's time on earth ended, she was assumed body and soul into heaven. The Assumption is her resurrection and, like that of her Son, a promise of our future bodily resurrection. It was a stroke of spiritual genius to choose the vision of the pregnant woman "clothed with the sun, with the moon under her feet, and on her head a crown of twelve stars" (Revelation 12:1) for the first reading for the feast of the Assumption. In a way, this was the first Marian vision in Church history. Coupled with the second reading about the resurrection of the body, we behold Mary in glory, a promise of our future and a confirmation of Christ's pledge: "Those who eat my flesh and drink my blood have eternal life, and I will raise them up on the last day" (John 6:54).

Jesus will keep his promise to give us eternal life and a resurrected body, provided we keep our faith in him and

Mary's Faith

The blessings so beautifully manifested in Mary's faith at the time of Christ appear again in many Marian shrines: Lourdes, Fátima, Czestochowa, Medjugorje, and Guadalupe, to name a few. In Nazareth, an angel appeared to Mary and called her to faith. In her subsequent appearances, Mary calls us to faith. She asks us to pray, which is an act of faith in God. She always invites us to do penance so that we may undergo a deeper conversion to Christ and a purification of our faith relationship to God.

Sometimes she requests that a church be built, where the central mystery of our faith, the Holy Eucharist, may be celebrated. Of the millions of pilgrims who flock to her shrines, there is virtually unanimous testimony that their faith has been strengthened and their prayer life deepened.

Our Holy Mother Mary inspires and urges countless pilgrims to imitate her historic "yes" of faith in the will of God. At Lourdes, one of the most famous sites of Marian apparitions, the daily experiences of the pilgrims are usually quiet, dignified, and devotional. This is nourished by the candlelight procession in the evening, accompanied by the soaring hymn *Immaculate Mary* that never fails to stir all hearts.

Another devotional moment happens in the daytime when there is an outdoor procession of the Blessed Sacrament in which the priest carries the monstrance that displays the real presence of Christ in the consecrated host. As he passes by the large number of pilgrims, many in wheelchairs or on stretchers, he blesses them with the Eucharist. It is a time of deep reverence, awe, adoration, and a yearning for healing that includes a faith that says, "Yes, Jesus, thy will be done."

Continued on next page

Continued from previous page

Hoping for a cure, many bathe in or touch the pool fed by the spring uncovered by St. Bernadette at the request of Mary. Extraordinary miracles sometimes happen. Sixty-four cures are duly recognized as authentic miracles. However, practically every pilgrim claims a renewal of faith. Wherever Mary is celebrated, she is turning people to faith in Christ, prayer to our Father and trust in the Holy Spirit, repentance of sins, and a special focus on the Mass and adoration of the Eucharist.

live out his love. Mary is our greatest ally in this adventure. Pilgrims at her shrines know this and praise Mary for her interest in our happiness and salvation. She was the woman of faith on earth and will teach us how to do it in our lives. Mary, Seat of Wisdom, pray for us.

For Reflection

1. What has been your life experience of Mary?
2. How has Mary helped your faith growth? How has she been a mother to you?
3. How have you witnessed Mary's influence on others? What has been the impact on them?

Prayer

Lord, we praise you for the many blessings you gave to Mary, your beloved mother. Show us how to relate more fruitfully to Mary, who then will help us get closer to you. Holy Spirit of our faith that is needed to be open to your message of salvation, put a living spark of that faith in our souls. Amen.

CHAPTER SIXTEEN

LAST THINGS

> *The Christian meaning of death is revealed in the light of the* Paschal mystery *of the death and resurrection of Christ in whom resides our only hope. The Christian who dies in Christ Jesus is "away from the body and at home with the Lord" (2 Cor 5:8).* — CCC, 1681 (EMPHASIS IN ORIGINAL)

In Robert Bolt's play *A Man for All Seasons*, St. Thomas More (1478-1535) reminds us that final judgment awaits each one of us. Death spares no one, neither king nor commoner. While the words Bolt puts on More's tongue are fictionalized, the ideas are not. Lord Chancellor of England under Henry VIII, More was beheaded for refusing to take an oath of loyalty to the king, which would have indicated his moral approval of the king's divorce from Katherine of Aragon and his remarriage to Anne Boleyn, as well as Henry's self-proclamation as head of the Church in England. More spent considerable time in prison, where he quietly pondered the meaning of life and death. He could have given in to Henry, left prison, and still retain sufficient fame to be remembered in the history books — though for less honorable reasons.

He was a "patron saint" of religious humanists who prized the intellectual life. But his devout faith surpassed the wit and learning that characterized his role as a sharp-minded lawyer, judge, and creative writer.

Religious motivation dominated his days in the Tower of London, as it had all his life. He bore witness to the will of God by taking seriously the words of an oath, which God would witness. If he were to lie, that would be perjury in the divine courtroom. He valued words and their meaning, especially when they implied a moral commitment. Dying would not terrorize him into telling lies and acting immorally. More faced his death courageously, saying, "I die the king's good servant, and God's first," and allegedly telling his executioner not to be afraid of performing his duty because the man was merely sending him to God.

More spent his final days in the Tower thinking of those he loved most: his God and his family. He lavished his love on his favorite daughter, Margaret. When she came to see him, he rushed past the guards to embrace her for the last time, saying: "Farewell, my dear, I shall pray for you and all my friends, that we may merrily meet in heaven."

More's example is one effective and inspiring way of preparing for death, which is really the art of living.

Young people seldom think about dying unless they have a life-threatening illness or have dangerous occupations, such as soldiers in time of war or police in rough neighborhoods of our cities, or face the death of a friend or family member. With life expectancy increasing, there is a natural tendency to put off thoughts of dying later and later. Even when people are actually in the course of a fatal illness, they often avoid its reality through the stages of denial, anger, bargaining, and depression before final acceptance, as Dr. Elisabeth Kübler-Ross first described in her 1969 book, *On Death and Dying*.

The fact is that our whole Christian life should be a preparation for life in the next world. Medieval writers often counseled people, "As you live so shall you die." If our lives are governed by the virtues of faith, hope, and love, as well as prudence, temperance, justice, and courage, we are growing in the art of living. If our prayer life moves us to greater union with God, the virtues will flourish in our life. If we learn how to live the Ten Commandments, we will know how the love of God and neighbor become practical for us.

When we consistently draw divine graces from the sacraments, we receive the supernatural gifts that make the art of living a constant joy, even in the midst of disappointments and suffering. The best way to die is to live exuberantly the life of God in a human context.

"Had you a good conscience, death would hold no terrors for you; even so, it were better to avoid sin than to escape death. If you are not ready to die today, will tomorrow find you better prepared?"[22]

— THOMAS À KEMPIS

Certain principles govern the art of dying:

♦ **The first principle is that it is better to think about death (even when we are young) than to deny or ignore it.** Facing death helps us to live each day to the fullest. The proper contemplation of death moves us to value our earthly lives, and it opens us to a religious faith in the hereafter. To ignore death tempts us to treat a future life as absurd and to cast a shadow over living. Taking some time now and then in thoughtful solitude leads us to appreciate our moral and spiritual worth.

♦ **The second principle is that it is better to think about the death of Jesus than to ignore it.** Why else does the Church place the crucifix before our eyes at every Mass? Why else does the Church give us Lent and Holy Week to focus our attention on the passion and death of Jesus? Why else does the Church give us the feast of the Exaltation of the Holy Cross on September 14? In contemplating the cross, we observe how Jesus accepted his death, how he saved us from our sins by becoming a wounded healer, and how his exemplary suffering and death (marked by words and acts of forgiveness) is a model for the art of dying for all of us.

♦ **The third principle is that part of dying is to fix our eyes on the prize, eternal life hereafter.** Jesus showed us that death is both the key to human fulfillment here and to ultimate joy hereafter. He helps us understand that an Easter person carries forward the Way of the Cross, just as he brought the scars of the Passion into resurrected life. Cross and Easter form one reality, even as death and immortality in the next life fuse into one event. Small wonder, then, that St. Paul envisions the sound of trumpets announcing our new life in Christ: "For the trumpet will sound, and the dead will be raised imperishable, and we will be changed" (1 Corinthians 15:52).

As we learn the art of dying, some basic truths about death need to be understood. We list them here for the sake of the record. Penetrating their meaning may be found in the *Catechism* (1020-1050):

1. **Death is the outcome of original sin.** "You may freely eat of every tree of the garden; but of the tree of the knowledge of good and evil you shall not eat, for in the day that you eat of it you shall die" (Genesis 2:16-17). "The wages of sin is death, but the free gift of God is eternal life in Christ Jesus our Lord" (Romans 6:23).

2. **Christ has conquered death by his death and resurrection.** "We have been buried with him by baptism into death, so that, just as Christ was raised from the dead by the glory of the Father, so we too might walk in newness of life" (Romans 6:4).

3. **Life is changed, not taken away.** "When the body of our earthly dwelling lies in death we gain an everlasting dwelling place in heaven" (Preface I for Christian Death).

4. **Our bodies will rise again.** "If the dead are not raised, then Christ has not been raised. If Christ has not been raised, your faith is futile and you are still in your sins" (1 Corinthians 15:16-17).

5. **At death, we face the particular judgment, in which we will enter heaven — either through a particular purification (purgatory) or immediately — or, tragically, hell.** This is illustrated by Christ's parable about the poor man Lazarus and the rich man as well as the account of the good thief on Calvary, where their destinies immediately after death are described (cf. CCC, 1021-1022).

6. At the end of time, the resurrection of the dead, both the just and unjust, will take place. In the presence of Christ, all human relationships with God will be revealed and the consequences made known: "The hour is coming when all who are in their graves will hear his voice and will come out — those who have done good, to the resurrection of life, and those who have done evil, to the resurrection of condemnation" (John 5:28-29). (See also Matthew 25:31-46, where Jesus describes the Last Judgment as a separation of the just from the unjust in terms of those who ministered to Christ in the hungry, naked, sick, prisoners, etc., and those who did not.)

7. The kingdom of God will be completely manifested. The saved, glorified in body and soul, will reign with Christ forever. There will be a new heaven and a new earth: "Then I saw a new heaven and a new earth; for the first heaven and the first earth had passed away, and the sea was no more. And I saw the holy city, the new Jerusalem, coming down out of heaven from God" (Revelation 21:1-2).

For Reflection

1. Have you thought about dying? Are you afraid to contemplate your death?
2. How can you prepare for your death by living fully?
3. Why are prayers for the sick and dying so important?

Prayer

Holy Mary, Mother of God, pray for us sinners, now and at the hour of our death. Amen.

SECTION TWO

LOVE FOR YOUR HEART

CHAPTER SEVENTEEN

THE PASCHAL MYSTERY AND FOUNTAINS OF SALVATION

> *For it is in the liturgy through which, especially in the divine sacrifice of the Eucharist, that "the work of our redemption is accomplished," and it is through the liturgy, especially, that the faithful are able to express in their lives and manifest to others the mystery of Christ and the real nature of the true Church.* — SACROSANCTUM CONCILIUM (CONSTITUTION ON THE SACRED LITURGY), 2

Francis Van Thuan (1928-2002) always ended the letters he wrote to his parents during his thirteen years in prison in Vietnam (nine in solitary confinement) with these words:

> Dear Mum and Dad, do not burden your hearts with sadness. I live each day united with the universal Church and Jesus' sacrifice. Pray that I have the courage and strength to always remain faithful to the Church and the Gospel, and to do God's will.[23]

The eldest of eight children in a devout Catholic family, Francis was ordained in 1953 and was appointed the first Vietnamese bishop of Nha Trang in 1967. After being named coadjutor archbishop (with rights of succession) to the archbishop of Saigon in 1975, he was arrested and imprisoned in northern Vietnam. After a number of years, he persuaded his captors to give him some bread and wine each month, and from then on he celebrated the Eucharist each day in his cell, retaining a small piece of Christ's sacramental Body in his shirt pocket next to his heart. With little to distract him, his attention was on God alone. After he was freed in 1988, he became an archbishop in Rome and worked for peace and justice around the world. Soon after being named a cardinal, he died in 2002.

On June 19, 2008, his youngest sister, Elizabeth Nguyen Thi Thu Hong, one of the speakers at the International Eucharistic Congress in Quebec City, noted this about her brother:

> Through his writings, and most particularly through his correspondence from prison, one clear fact emerges: Francis' life was firmly rooted in an extraordinary union with the living God through the Eucharist, his only strength. It was also to him the most beautiful prayer, and the best way to give thanks and sing the glory of God. May this former prisoner who experienced heaven's harmony, love, and life to the fullest in the desolation of his prison cell continue to guide us so that we can be like the disciples of Emmaus who called out, "Lord, remain with us and feed us with your body."[24]

For us, as for Francis Van Thuan, each liturgy enacts Christ's Paschal Mystery. It is a "mystery" because it is an act of the divine Persons of the Trinity. The term "mystery" respects the transcendence of God, who reveals his actions at liturgy. At liturgy, we praise the Father from whom all blessings flow into our lives. We adore the Son of God, who brings us his salvation through all the sacraments. We worship the Holy Spirit, who makes present the graces of God and sanctifies us during our participation in the holy sacraments.

> "The late Cardinal Nguyen Van Thuan, a prisoner for thirteen years, nine of them spent in solitary confinement, has left us a precious little book: *Prayers of Hope.* During thirteen years in jail, in a situation of seemingly utter hopelessness, the fact that he could listen and speak to God became for him an increasing power of hope, which enabled him, after his release, to become for people all over the world a witness to hope — to that great hope which does not wane even in the nights of solitude."[25]
>
> — POPE BENEDICT XVI

The Paschal Mystery is "paschal" because it makes present the greatest act in salvation history — Christ's death and resurrection, by which we are saved from sin and given a share in divine life. The Paschal Mystery is a process whereby we are gradually transformed into the mystery of divine life. The Father blesses us with his Son's saving acts. The Son actively draws us into his dying and rising, a cycle that continues for all of us as we die constantly to sin and rise always to a closer life in God. The Holy Spirit fulfills in us the words of the Father: "Be holy, for I am holy" (Leviticus 11:45).

What happened in salvation history is made available to us through the Church and the seven sacraments. The Trinity is involved in the ministry of the Incarnate Word. The Father planned to save us. The Son, Jesus Christ, actually saved us. The Holy Spirit confirmed and sustained the work of the Son in the lives of those he formed and the Church he established. The Spirit continues the process of sanctification of people today. The New Testament, produced and interpreted by the Church, provides us with the historical record of how all this happened.

The sacraments make present today the work of Jesus. The seven sacraments are: Baptism, Confirmation,

Lord of Heaven in a Shirt Pocket

"In prison with the Eucharistic Jesus in their midst, Christian and non-Christian prisoners slowly received the grace to understand that each present moment of their lives in the most inhuman conditions can be united with the supreme sacrifice of Jesus and lifted up as an act of solemn adoration of God the Father. I would like to quote these words of my brother: 'I am happy here in my cell where white mushrooms are growing on my mat, because you are here with me, because you want me to live here with you. Now I speak no more. It's your turn to speak to me, Jesus. I am listening to you.'

"Every time I read this, I can't help imagining my brother, sitting in his dark cell, facing complete emptiness, but gently smiling as he always did, even during his last days, and holding tightly and lovingly to his shirt pocket where the Lord of heaven rested."[26]

— ELIZABETH NGUYEN THI THU HONG,
CARDINAL VAN THUAN'S SISTER

Eucharist, Reconciliation, Anointing of the Sick, Holy Orders, and Matrimony. The sacraments are effective signs of grace. This means that each sacrament, by the power of the Holy Spirit, creates in us the specific work of God intended by the sacrament.

In each sacrament, we come into direct contact with God. All of the loving and compassionate energies of the Father's abundant blessings, the Son's powerful redeeming process, and the Holy Spirit's endless fountain of divine love are offered to us in every sacrament experience. This is true of sacraments we only receive once — Baptism, Confirmation, Holy Orders, Matrimony (usually) — for their impact affects us all our life. Obviously, the sacraments we experience more often — Eucharist, Reconciliation, and Anointing — have an immediate, noticeable effect on our life.

But these gifts from God only transform us if we are receptive. At liturgy, we need "ears to hear" in faith the sacred words of God spoken to us. We need "eyes to see" in faith the divine realities made visible in rituals and symbols. St. Thomas Aquinas wrote, "Whatever is received from God is received according to the capacity of the receiver." God does not force-feed his gifts on us. If, sadly, we have narrow, tight little hearts, we confine what God can give us. If we have stretched our hearts grandly with a wide-open welcome to God's life-changing graces, God joyfully fills every inch of our souls.

As we shall see in our reflection on the Eucharist, it is in this sacrament that we are most regularly and enthusiastically fed with the bread of God, the Body and Blood of Christ. Many seekers for spiritual nourishment — even within the Church — look everywhere for this divine life, yet somehow fail to appreciate the Eucharist, the summit

Signs and Symbols

"The liturgical celebration involves signs and symbols relating to creation (candles, water, fire), human life (washing, anointing, breaking bread) and the history of salvation (the rites of the Passover). Integrated into the world of faith and taken up by the power of the Holy Spirit, these cosmic elements, human rituals, and gestures of remembrance of God become bearers of the saving and sanctifying action of Christ."

— CCC, 1189

and source of the Christian life. For some, it seems too simple, too obvious — yet nothing is less obvious than the obvious. There is gold on our altar and tabernacle. Why settle for lead?

The celebration of the liturgy follows a regular pattern called the Liturgical Year.

From Advent to Pentecost, the liturgy provides us with the opportunity to celebrate the mysteries of Christ's incarnation, life, death, resurrection, ascension, and sending of the Spirit. By spreading out the events for about six months every year, the Church gives us a coherent celebration of Christ's life that does more than merely invite us to imitate the morals he teaches or the example he displays.

When an event of Christ's history is presented in liturgy, it is not just a Scripture class. Because this takes place at worship, the Holy Spirit provides us with the special graces proper to the aspect of Christ's teaching and example that is celebrated. In these liturgies, Christ invites us to identify with him in his healings, teachings, prayers, works of love, suffering, death, and resurrection. Identification is more than imitation. In identification, the Holy Spirit transforms us little by little into Christ. Imitation has its value, but it tends to be external, whereas what we need is an inner change caused by God.

The same principle applies for the remainder of the year, called Ordinary Time, when we strive to live out the implications of the events of Christ's life in our own life. During this time, we have the cycle of the feasts and memorials of Mary, the apostles, martyrs, virgins, confessors, and other saints. On these joyful days, we share in the life-changing power of Jesus seen in this cloud of witnesses. Mary and the saints show us that the promises of God really come true. The Liturgical Year is the Holy Spirit's annual training period of our interior life. The process is not over after one year; it lasts until we die. Always linked to the Eucharist, this process is a transformation that can make us saints if we open ourselves to its remarkable power and practice its meaning in everyday life.

For Reflection

1. In what ways are you aware of the sanctifying power of the liturgy?
2. How does Cardinal Van Thuan's prison story affect your appreciation of the Holy Eucharist?
3. How can you best enter into the life-changing events of the Liturgical Year?

Prayer

Jesus, you in me and I in you.

— Cardinal Van Thuan's prison prayer

CHAPTER EIGHTEEN

REBIRTH IN WATER AND SPIRIT

> *John answered them, "I baptize with water. Among you stands one whom you do not know, the one who is coming after me; I am not worthy to untie the thong of his sandal." This took place in Bethany across the Jordan where John was baptizing.*
> — JOHN 1:26-28

It is very likely that as a youth John the Baptist joined the Essene monastery of Qumran. The Dead Sea Scrolls tell us a great deal about this holy community that lived by the shores of the Dead Sea. The members saw themselves as the fulfillment of Isaiah's prophecy of a voice crying out for spiritual renewal from their desert pulpit. John absorbed their message, but claimed that he was actually that voice sent by God and preached, "Prepare the way of the Lord."

At Qumran, the members prized prayer and fasting and an ascetical lifestyle that appealed to John. More to our point, John was impressed by their practice of ritual baths — or baptisms — to symbolize their quest for moral purity. John transformed their insight into a single water cleansing, a baptism in water to prepare for the messianic baptism in water and the Holy Spirit. In time, John left the comfort of their community to preach to the world about penance and baptism, to prepare for the Messiah.

His preaching and baptisms by the Jordan River attracted great crowds. Then one day Jesus came and requested baptism. John protested, "I need to be baptized by you." Jesus said, "Let it be so now; for it is proper for us in this way to fulfill all righteousness" (Matthew 3:14, 15). Blending into the mass of sinners along the banks of the Jordan, Jesus carried the weight of all human sin into the watery tomb of the river. In his baptism, Jesus anticipated bearing the burden of the cross to save us. In that watery cavern, he symbolically began the conquest of the evil one. Then rising out of the river he gave us a forecast of his resurrection and the triumph over evil. Then the heavens were opened and the voice of the Father declared that Jesus is his Son and that we should listen to him. The Holy Spirit appeared in the form of a dove of peace, confirming the Father's union with the Son's mission. This Trinitarian vision at the Jordan reminds us that the Trinity is present at every baptism, for it is in their name that we receive the sacrament.

> "Our Savior came to be baptized, so that through the cleansing waters of baptism he might restore the old man to new life, heal our sinful nature, and clothe us with unfailing holiness."
>
> — ANTIPHON FOR THE CANTICLE OF MARY, EVENING PRAYER I, FEAST OF THE BAPTISM OF THE LORD

Baptism, Confirmation, and the Eucharist are the welcoming sacraments, the rites of initiation into the community of the Church, the Body of Christ. Baptism is our entrance into the kingdom of God, a kingdom of love, justice, peace, and salvation from sin. It is the sacrament by which we are incorporated into the Body of Christ by a bond of unity that joins together all who are transformed by the Spirit. Through the power of the living Word of God, Baptism makes us sharers in the very life of God as his adopted sons and daughters. With the three pourings of water, accompanied by the words "in the name of the Father, and of the Son, and of the Holy Spirit," we are cleansed from all sin and are welcomed into communion with the members of the Trinity. The Scripture readings, the prayers of the community, and our own triple profession of faith prepare the candidates for these gifts. Baptism produces all these blessings through the power of Christ's death and resurrection. We die to sin with Christ, and we rise to a share in divine life with him.

Baptism is not like a graduation diploma. It is not the end but instead the beginning of a relationship with Christ and the members of his Church. We have joined the family of God with all its benefits and responsibilities. The faith that brought us to the font must be developed and enriched by regular participation in the worship life of the Church, a commitment to live out the two greatest commandments of Christ — love of God and love of neighbor — as well as the Ten Commandments, and a resolve to acquire the virtues of a Christian. We promise to make prayer as natural to us as breathing, and we beg God to show us how to trust in him and do his will. Because of our baptism, we try, with God's graces, to grow spiritually as individuals, as members of a family and a parish, and as citizens of a society. Linked to these goals is a resolution to be a lifelong learner of the meaning of our faith.

While most of us were baptized as infants, in the case of adults there is a preparation process known as the Rite of Christian Initiation of Adults (RCIA). This process includes the Rite of Election, religious instruction in the truths of the Catholic faith, rituals that mark the progress of the candidates, and the prayers and companionship of the parish community. The journey reaches its summit at the Easter Vigil Mass on Holy Saturday night, where Baptism, Confirmation, and the Eucharist are received. (Baptized members of other faiths receive Confirmation and Eucharist.) This joyful experience extends throughout the seven weeks of Easter up to Pentecost, where the new Catholics receive in depth the spiritual meanings of what they have received.

"[Confirmation] roots the recipient more deeply in divine sonship, binds him more firmly to Christ and to the Church and reinvigorates the gifts of the Holy Spirit in his soul. It gives a special strength to witness to the Christian faith."

— COMPENDIUM, 268

The New Testament reports the action of the Holy Spirit helping Jesus in his messianic mission. The Spirit anoints Jesus for his public ministry during his Jordan baptism. In his sermon to the people in the Nazareth synagogue, Jesus applies to himself the words of Isaiah: "The Spirit of the Lord is upon me" (Luke 4:18). He promised his disciples that the Spirit would strengthen them in tough times. After his resurrection, Jesus tells them that they will feel the power of God and become his witnesses to the world when the Holy Spirit descends on them, which happened at Pentecost. Throughout the Acts of the Apostles, there are accounts of the remarkable influence of the Holy Spirit on their preaching, their enthusiasm for the faith, and their courage in standing up for Christ, even in the face of torture and death — a stark contrast to their fear and timidity before receiving the Holy Spirit. Not only did they receive the Spirit, they also began imparting the Holy Spirit to others by the laying on of hands. Repeatedly they gave others the gift of the Spirit. The Church has always understood this as the origin of the Sacrament of Confirmation, which continues the graces of Pentecost in our Church today.

Generally, we identify Confirmation with Christian courage, but the Holy Spirit is also a unifier, a source of unity for the Church that historically has faced so many occasions of division. As the personalized love that exists between the Father and the Son, the Holy Spirit breathes into the Church the love that unites the members. Material concerns often divide us, but the unifying love of the Spirit forms us into a community.

Both Baptism and Confirmation confer a "character," a spiritual branding, that reflects God's unswerving fidelity to the recipients and calls them to an equal loyalty to God; this permanence means that these sacraments cannot be repeated.

One of the difficulties of receiving Baptism and Confirmation only once is that we forget the influence they are meant to exert on our lives. We need to renew the commitments associated with these sacraments. Each time we enter our parish church we dip our hands in the holy water font and bless ourselves "in the name of the Father, and of the Son, and of the Holy Spirit." This little custom can be a chance to renew our dedication to God by saying, "Dear God, with this blessing I renew my baptismal promises." Then, when you kneel down at your pew, say the Apostles' Creed as an act of faith and ask God to help you to grow personally as a Christian and communally as a member of the parish, and as a productive member of society. Decide again to be a "kingdom of God" Catholic, seeking love, mercy, justice, and salvation for yourself and others. Repent your sins and faults. Seek conversion of heart. Make Christ your rock, your stronghold, your ideal.

For Reflection

1. In what ways can you live out the renewal of your baptismal and confirmation promises?
2. If you attend a baptism or confirmation at Easter Vigil, what can this do for your own faith development?
3. Who in your parish is attending RCIA? How can they help motivate you to self-evaluation and turning over a new leaf in your spiritual journey?

Prayer

Renewal of Baptismal Promises

I reject Satan and all his works and all his empty promises.

I believe in God, the Father almighty, Creator of heaven and earth.

I believe in Jesus Christ, his only Son, our Lord, who was born of the Virgin Mary, was crucified, died, and was buried, rose from the dead, and is now seated at the right hand of the Father.

I believe in the Holy Spirit, the holy Catholic Church, the communion of saints, the forgiveness of sins, the resurrection of the body, and life everlasting.

Amen.

— ADAPTED FROM THE VIGIL MASS OF EASTER

CHAPTER NINETEEN

"IN REMEMBRANCE OF ME"

> *When he had given thanks, he broke it and said, "This is my body that is for you. Do this in remembrance of me." In the same way he took the cup also, after supper, saying, "This cup is the new covenant in my blood. Do this, as often as you drink it, in remembrance of me."* — 1 Corinthians 11:24-25

At the 2008 International Eucharistic Congress in Quebec City, Pope Benedict XVI said: "I urge priests especially to give due honor to the Eucharistic rite, and I ask all the faithful to respect the role of each individual, both priest and lay, in the Eucharistic action."[27] His words echo the words and deeds of the saints over the centuries. In the left transept of St. Peter's Basilica, there is a statue of St. Norbert (1080-1134) holding high the Blessed Sacrament. He is standing on the neck of the heretic Berengar of Tours, who denied Christ's real presence in the Eucharist.

After his ordination to the priesthood, Norbert obtained papal permission to preach in the villages and towns of early medieval France. He preached a call to peace to the warlords and pastoral reform to the clergy. His missions always included the celebration of Mass, at which he reintroduced the practice of the homily, which had been omitted, and restored faith in the real presence of Jesus in the Eucharist, which had been weakened by Berengar's false teachings.

Eventually, he founded the Canons Regular of Premontre (the Norbertines) to establish the spiritual renewal of the priesthood and institute a renewed reverence for the celebration of Mass.

Within four years of his new foundation, he received an appeal from the bishop of Antwerp. Twelve priests of the collegiate Church and monastery of St. Michael's had adopted the false view of the Eucharist and had to be removed. The bishop asked Norbert to send twelve of his priests to bring the people back to the true faith in the Mass and the priesthood. This event is remembered in the cathedral of Antwerp, where the full sweep of the stained glass windows on the north wall picture a procession of the Blessed Sacrament, with Norbert carrying the monstrance.

Norbert's approach to authentic faith in the Eucharist was practical. He insisted that the altar and sanctuary be immaculate, that the priests be diligent in awesome respect for the Eucharist and reverence for the rituals of the Mass, and that the people be trained to do the same. He helped clergy and laity to know that the Mass is a treasure of the Church.

"We must go back again and again to the Last Supper on Holy Thursday, where we were given a pledge of the mystery of our redemption on the cross. The Last Supper is the locus of the nascent Church, the womb containing the Church of every age. In the Eucharist, Christ's sacrifice is constantly renewed. Pentecost is constantly renewed." [28]

— POPE BENEDICT XVI

Scripture contains a vivid tapestry of texts that point to and describe the First Eucharist on Holy Thursday in the Upper Room. The Gospels of Matthew, Mark, and Luke as well as 1 Corinthian 11 report Christ's words instituting the Eucharist. John's Gospel does not have the words of institution but instead devotes a lengthy description of the meaning of the Eucharist in chapter six. There we hear Jesus say that he is the "living bread" come down from heaven, and that we are called to eat his flesh and drink his blood in order to receive his eternal life now and the resurrection of our bodies on the last day. The bread would become his Body and the wine would become his Blood in the sacrament. John develops this challenging message over and over and does not dilute it when a number of Jesus' listeners say they cannot accept it.

All four Gospels report Christ's miracle of the multiplication of the loaves and Matthew and Mark describe the occasion twice. This multiplication of bread is a prophecy of the Eucharistic bread that will become Christ's Body, just as the abundance of wine at the Cana wedding miracle foreshadows the Eucharistic wine that will become the Blood of Christ.

In the Book of Revelation, the numerous scenes of the heavenly liturgy, with choirs chanting the glory of God and praising the victory of the Lamb of God, are revelations of what is behind the Eucharistic liturgies on earth. Put another way, the author is telling us that heaven is present at every Mass. Did not Jesus say in John 6 that in the Eucharist he would give us eternal life? Lastly, the Letter to the Hebrews gives us an extensive meditation on the priesthood of Jesus Christ and the sacrificial quality of the liturgy as it appears today in our Mass and in the ordained priesthood.

Moreover, the Old Testament prophetically contributed to the First Eucharist. Jesus and his apostles in the Upper Room sat down at a Jewish Passover meal, where the foods on the table represented the details of the slavery in Egypt and the sacrificial lamb in the center of the table recalled God's plan to save the firstborn by the blood of a sacrificed lamb. When Jesus consecrated the wine, he used the Jewish language of covenant in a new covenant and therefore perfectly fulfilled God's covenant with Israel at Sinai.

At the beginning of the First Eucharist, Jesus led the apostles in Psalm 136, a hymn of thanksgiving for the "mighty deeds of God" in salvation history to which they all sang, in line after line, "For his mercy endures forever!" Little did the apostles realize that a few minutes later Christ the Lord would create the mightiest deed of all: the institution of the Sacrament of the Holy Eucharist that would carry the saving power of his forthcoming death

The Sacrifice of the Mass

A sacrificed lamb was the centerpiece of the Passover meal. Two apostles had purchased the lamb at the Temple and had given it to a priest to be sacrificed. The priest slew the lamb, poured out the blood, and said the prayers of offering. Then a portion was burned on the Altar of Holocausts and the remainder given back to the apostles for their Passover feast. Because of this, the Eucharist is a "sacrificial meal," not just a friendship supper, as indeed our Mass is a sacrifice as well as a Communion meal. Moreover, the real Lamb of God is the Lord Jesus, who is the host of the supper.

and resurrection for the rest of history to our altars and tabernacles and hearts.

The First Eucharist is a sacrament of salvation from sin and a communion in divine life. The sacrament on Thursday signified Christ's saving sacrifice on Good Friday and his saving resurrection on Easter Sunday. Why else did Jesus say: *This is my body that is to be given up (on the cross) for you.... This is the cup of my blood that will be shed (on the cross) for the forgiveness of your sins.* Jesus told them: *Do this in memory of me.* And so they did. Every Mass since then makes present Christ's death that saves us from sin and his resurrection that gives a share in his divine life and love.

Taking Part in the Mystery of Faith

"The Church, therefore, earnestly desires that Christ's faithful, when present at this mystery of faith, should not be there as strangers or silent spectators. On the contrary, through a good understanding of the rites and prayers they should take part in the sacred action, conscious of what they are doing, with devotion and full collaboration. They should be instructed by God's word, and be nourished at the table of the Lord's Body. They should give thanks to God. Offering the immaculate victim, not only through the hands of the priest but also with him, they should learn to offer themselves. Through Christ, the Mediator, they should be drawn day by day into ever more perfect union with God and each other, so that finally God may be all in all."

— *SACROSANCTUM CONCILIUM* (CONSTITUTION ON THE SACRED LITURGY), 48

At Mass, we are encouraged to do more than offer the Father the sacrifice of his Son; we are expected to offer the sacrifice of our lives as well. St. Paul taught this practice to the Romans: "I appeal to you therefore, brothers and sisters, by the mercies of God, to present your bodies as a living sacrifice, holy and acceptable to God, which is your spiritual worship" (Romans 12:1).

We have a tendency to love ourselves more than others. Jesus used that fact to command us to love others as we love ourselves. Christ calls us to self-giving sacrifice, which is a way to understand how to offer ourselves at Mass. The sending prayer at the end of Mass challenges us to go forth to love and serve the Lord, and others, as we love ourselves.

At the First Eucharist, Jesus washed the feet of his disciples and then told them he expected them to serve others in the same way. Loving service to others must be an essential outcome of participating in the Eucharist. We do not want to leave the church as Judas did and go out and betray Christ. Nor should we walk out the door and immediately deny Jesus by exploiting people, ignoring our children, manipulating our spouse, or treating people at work with arrogance, deceit, or indifference.

Throughout all of Church history, we have the example of men and women who actually gave up their lives in imitation of Christ. Their supreme sacrifice was a profound way of living the Sacrifice of the Mass. Because God loves us, he associates us with the great adventure of the salvation of the Lord. Our mission is to love. That was the lesson of the First Eucharist, and of the most recent Mass you attended.

For Reflection

1. What do you remember about your First Communion? How does it compare to your most recent Communion?
2. If someone asks you what the Mass is, how will you respond?
3. In what ways can we think less of what we get out of Mass and concentrate more on what we bring to the Eucharist?

Prayer

Lord, who at thy first Eucharist did pray
That all thy Church might be forever one,
Grant us at every Eucharist to say
With longing heart and soul, "Thy will be done."
O may we all one bread, one body be,
Through this blest Sacrament of Unity.

— WILLIAM H. TURTON

CHAPTER TWENTY

CORPUS CHRISTI

> *"I am the living bread that came down from heaven. Whoever eats of this bread will live forever.... Those who eat my flesh and drink my blood have eternal life ... [and they] abide in me, and I in them."* — JOHN 6:51, 54, 56

The seed that blossomed into the feast of Corpus Christi was planted by St. Juliana of Mt. Cornillon (1193-1258). From her early days as a nun in Liège, Belgium, she experienced a call to adoration of the Blessed Sacrament, while at the same time serving as a nurse in the convent-sponsored hospital. She began to have repeated visions of a white moon with one dark spot. She prayed for an interpretation of this vision and was rewarded by a vision of Jesus, who told her that the dark spot represented the absence of a special feast in honor of the Blessed Sacrament.

While there was already a feast of the Eucharist on Holy Thursday, its focus was on the events of the Passion of Christ. Sister Juliana heard Jesus say that there was need of a Eucharistic feast that also focused on his resurrection, both in the Mass and in the reserved, consecrated Hosts in the tabernacle. This devotion would extend the blessings of the Mass and increase people's faith in the Eucharist. The Church should then also encourage adoration of the reserved presence of Jesus.

After a number of humiliating setbacks, Sister Juliana (who was canonized by Pope Pius IX in 1869) persuaded the local bishop and his archdeacon Jacques Pantaléon (later to become Pope Urban IV) to establish the feast of Corpus Christi for their diocese in 1246, on the Thursday after Trinity Sunday.

When Pantaléon became pope, he was told about a miracle that happened to a priest who doubted Christ's presence in the Eucharist. While this priest was celebrating Mass, after the consecration, the Blood of Jesus flowed from the Host and spread over the linen cloth of the corporal. The congregation saw the miracle and rejoiced. Informed and assured of the authenticity of the miracle, and recalling Sister Juliana's vision, the pope enshrined the corporal in the Cathedral of Orvieto and decreed that the feast of Corpus Christ be observed by the whole Church in 1264. Pope Urban appointed St. Thomas Aquinas to write the text of the feast for the Mass and the Liturgy of the Hours. Today the feast is widely celebrated with a Eucharistic procession, often through the streets surrounding parish churches. Many Catholics are familiar with the Latin hymns *Tantum Ergo*, *Adoro Te*, and *Pange Lingua* that were written for this feast.

"This food which no hunger can expel, this is the bread which the Spirit has baked in a holy fire. This is a liquid which no thirst can destroy. This is the wine which the grape of the Virgin's womb has brought forth."

— MATTHEW OF RIEVAULX

The religious faith of our Catholic people has always found ways to express various kinds of piety that surround the Church's sacraments. Veneration of relics, pilgrimages to shrines, the Stations of the Cross, the Rosary, the wearing of medals and scapulars, the recitation of popular prayers, and Corpus Christi processions are among the many customs that can strengthen people's faith in the great mysteries of faith of the Church. Pope John Paul II referred to their importance when he said that, with proper pastoral discernment, "certain acts of piety … could serve very well to help people advance towards knowledge of the mystery of Christ."[29]

No form of popular piety surpasses adoration of the Eucharist. In every Mass, the priest bends his knee three times to adore the Eucharist: at the Consecration, to the Body of Christ and to his precious Blood, and just before receiving Communion. In every Mass, the congregation kneels in adoration of Christ made present, from the Consecration to the Our Father and again just before Communion. We adore Christ by bowing to him in the Host just before receiving him.

These moments of adoration at Mass were training sessions for private adoration of Christ in the Eucharist in times past. Popular piety understood instinctively the need to extend the privileged experience of the Mass to prayer time before the tabernacle or the exposition of the Blessed Sacrament.

Other customs call for adoring Jesus truly present in the tabernacle and a meditative silence before him while waiting for Mass to start. Alas, this custom presently has been replaced with noisy conversation. In former times, the period after Communion was quiet while the people knelt in adoration, closing their eyes to attend to Christ and privately commune with him. But now the singing and other musical distractions often divert our adoring attention away from Christ. Then there is the rush after Mass to the parking lot to get home. Good liturgy calls for brief periods of silence to help all of us focus on God and to catch our breath in the midst of the rituals.

Bishop Arthur Serratelli of Paterson, New Jersey, states the problem vividly:

> Certain settings demand their own particular etiquette. Dress at a wedding reception differs from dress at a sports event. Conversation in a bar is louder than in a funeral home. The more we realize we are coming into the presence of God in church, the more respectful and reverent our whole person becomes. Chewing gum in Church, loud talking, beach attire, and immodest dress simply do not belong! In church we need to cultivate a sense of God who is present to us. This is why we are called to observe moments of silence, both before Mass begins and during Mass. Liturgy is much more than our joining together. It is our opening ourselves to God. By our singing and praying, we respond to the God who addresses us in liturgy. A constant torrent of words and songs filling every space in the liturgy does not leave the heart the space it needs to rest quietly in the divine presence.[30]

One may conclude that parishes need to help parishioners regain the moments of adoration that already exist at Mass — before, during, and after. To heighten Eucharistic awareness, some parishes sponsor the Forty Hours devotion. Others have added a Corpus Christi procession throughout the neighborhood. Many parishes have re-

Archbishop Sheen's Holy Hour

Archbishop Fulton Sheen (1895–1979) committed himself to a holy hour before the Blessed Sacrament every day. He often spoke about its value in his retreat talks, his sermons for days of recollection, and his writings. We summarize here several of his reasons for this devotion:

1. Because this is time spent in the presence of our Lord himself. If faith is alive, no other reason is needed.

2. Because in our busy life it takes considerable time to shake off the worldly cares that cling to our souls like dust.

3. Because this keeps a balance between the spiritual and the practical. Thanks to the hour with our Lord, our meditations and resolutions pass from the conscious to the subconscious and then become motives of our actions.

4. Because it will restore our lost spiritual vitality. "It reduces our liability to temptation and weakness.... Our will becomes disposed to goodness with little conscious effort on our part."

5. Because an hour with Our Lord follows the experience of the disciples on the road to Emmaus. We begin by walking with Our Lord but our eyes are "held fast" and we do not recognize him. Next he converses with our souls as we read the Scriptures. The third stage is one of sweet intimacy, as when he sat down with them. The fourth stage is the full dawning of the mystery of the Eucharist. Our eyes are "opened" and we recognize him. Finally, we reach the point where we do not want to leave. As we arise, we ask: "Were not our hearts burning within us while he was talking to us on the road, while he was opening the scriptures to us?" (Luke 24:32).[31]

stored the tabernacle to prominence as recommended by the *Catechism*: "The tabernacle should be located in an especially worthy place in the church and should be constructed in such a way that it emphasizes and manifests the truth of the real presence of Christ in the Blessed Sacrament" (CCC, 1379).

Adoration outside of Mass may take the form of a short visit or a longer period of adoration, such as a Holy Hour. Hundreds of parishes have started Eucharistic Adoration either during the day or perpetually. Many pastors report the positive effects this has on the whole parish, especially an increase in weekly Mass attendance, family stability, stronger marriages, and in some cases a growth in vocations to the priesthood and religious life. When significant numbers of parishioners are involved in contemplative prayer before the Blessed Sacrament, the results are palpable in the intensity of the faith life of the broader parish membership.

Reflection Questions

1. How would you judge the quality of reverence and the sense of the sacred at the Masses you attend? If it is good, what accounts for that? If it needs improvement, what would you suggest?
2. How strong is your faith in the real presence of Christ in the Eucharist? What would you say to someone who denies this truth of our faith?
3. What can you do to help people recover a sense of the sacred?

Prayer

[Dear God,]
In this great sacrament you feed your people
and strengthen them in holiness
so that the family of mankind
may come to walk in the light of one faith,
in one communion of love.
We come then to this wonderful sacrament
to be fed at your table
and grow into the likeness of the risen Christ.

— FROM THE PREFACE FOR THE SOLEMNITY OF THE BODY
AND BLOOD OF CHRIST (CORPUS CHRISTI)

CHAPTER TWENTY-ONE

"FORGIVE ME — I HAVE SINNED"

> *When he saw their faith, he said, "Friend, your sins are forgiven you."* — LUKE 5:20

Among all of Christ's parables, none is more touching than the Prodigal Son (Luke 15:11-32). The only time that Scripture shows God running is in this parable when the father runs toward his son with arms open and a heart overflowing with forgiveness: "His father saw him and *was filled with compassion; he ran* and put his arms around him and kissed him" (Luke 15:20, emphasis added). The father of the boy is an image of our Father of Mercies. Jesus is telling us what his Father is really like. In this story, the father did three things:

♦ **He hugged his son.** In fact, he did it with such warmth and affection that he smothered any attempt of his son to get out any of the words of his "confession of sins and repentance speech." I read about a psychologist who reported that he once heard a family court judge say that of all the hundreds of juvenile offenders and their parents who came before him, he never saw a parent put a protective arm around a youngster's shoulders.

♦ **He put shoes on his son's feet.** In biblical times, only free people wore shoes. The slaves went barefoot. The same was true of black slaves in America. No wonder they sang in church that all of God's children have shoes. The father brought his son into full and equal membership with everyone in the house by giving him shoes.

♦ **He placed a ring on his son's finger.** Almost certainly this was a ring with the family seal on it. This means he gave his son the right to seal papers and letters that dealt with important transactions in family affairs — something like being co-signers to a checking account. He gave his son a sign of trust.

Like the father in the story, our heavenly Father offers us holistic reconciliation, a reunion with him that is both generous and restorative.

"The more the human conscience ... loses its sense of the very meaning of the word 'mercy' ... the more the Church has the right and duty to appeal to the God of mercy 'with loud cries' (Hebrews 5:7)."[32]

— POPE JOHN PAUL II

On Good Friday, Jesus sacrificed himself to save the world from sins and win for everyone a share in his divine life. His last words were filled with mercy and forgiveness. What was his first major deed after his resurrection? It took place on Easter Sunday night. As we read in the twentieth chapter of John's Gospel, the apostles were still huddled in fear behind closed doors. They needed a divine shot in the arm and received more than they ever imagined. The Risen Jesus suddenly appeared to them and calmed them down by saying, "Peace be with you" (John 20:19). After showing them the scars of the wounds in the hands and side of his glorified body, Jesus filled them with the joy of recognizing him.

In the beginning of the Genesis Creation story, God breathed his spirit on the dark chaos, and with the appearance of light he started the first creation. Now in the Upper Room, Jesus breathed on the chaotic and fearful apostles. He told them that his breath was the creative power of the Spirit, the beginning of a new creation: "Receive the Holy Spirit." What was the purpose? The forgiveness of sins. He said, "If you forgive the sins of any, they are forgiven them; if you retain the sins of any, they are retained" (John 20:22-23).

He provided the world with the Sacrament of Reconciliation by giving the apostles and their successors, the bishops and their priests, the power to forgive sins. God is rich in mercy, and the Sacrament of Reconciliation is living proof of his concern to apply the fruits of his Paschal Mystery to heal the souls of sinners. The Holy Spirit works through this sacrament and the ministry of the Church and her priests to bring us forgiveness of sins.

If we do not believe we have sinned, we will never go to confession. The reason why confession lines are so short or nonexistent is because of a steep decline in our awareness of our sinfulness. In his book *Whatever Became of Sin?* psychiatrist Karl Menninger wrote that modern people attribute what used to be called sin to psychological sickness or to social forces over which they have no control. But neither the language of therapy nor the explanations from social forces is an adequate substitute for describing the reality of sin. We are not completely at the mercy of outside forces or inner compulsions. As images of God, we have the capacity for goodness, but as heirs to fallen humanity we are inclined to evil. All too often we have a wrecked relationship with God. Instead of trying to improve our union with God by praying, practicing virtues, benefiting from the Sacrament of Reconciliation, and imploring the help of the Holy Spirit, we wander away from our promised homeland and attempt to live without God.

> "If Jesus is your center and Lord and you fail him he will forgive you. Your career can't die for your sins. You might say 'If I were a Christian I'd be going around pursued by guilt all the time.' But we *all* are being pursued by guilt because we must have an identity and there must be some standard to live up to by which we get that identity. Whatever you base your life on you have to live up to *that*. Jesus is the one Lord you can live for who died for you — breathed his last breath for you. Does that sound oppressive?"[33]
>
> — TIMOTHY KELLER

We are taught that sins are acts that break the Ten Commandments. But it is breaking the First Commandment — which is another version of Christ's two greatest commandments, love of God and neighbor — that is the fundamental sin. The key insight of the First Commandment is: Adore the true God. Don't worship false gods. The other nine commandments illustrate those other gods: profanity, family betrayal, killing, stealing, lying, sexual infidelity, lies, lust, and greed. All these acts injure a relationship with God, just as marital infidelity erodes spousal love.

What we need is continual repentance — conversion from sinfulness and continual growth in real union with God. The Holy Spirit will then convince us of our inclination to sin, convict us of the sins we commit, and convert us to grace and love and console us in the process. We

A Good Christian

"Remember, a good Christian is not someone who doesn't ever sin, but someone who repents every time he does. That means that, ultimately, the definition of a successful life is one in which we repent *one more time than we sin*.... We have to rise up whenever we fall and continue the fight. If we fall a thousand times — if we fall *ten thousand times* — we should muster the boldness to say to God:

> Lord, I know I did something terrible and I feel awful. But I'm not going to let it discourage me. I'm sorry. I'm going to try not to do it again. I may break the world record for committing this particular sin, but I'm also going to break the record for repenting of it! And God, I promise to do my best to forgive everyone who offends me. After all, if you can forgive me after all the times I've disobeyed you, I can at least try to be merciful to others.

"This kind of prayer is music to God's ears. He doesn't just like it, he *loves* it.... You may sin grievously, time and time again, but he won't be able to do anything but smile as he pronounces his merciful judgment on your soul: 'Slate cleaned, door opened, burden lifted, sins forgiven.' "[34]

— ANTHONY DE STEPHANO

must remember that only God can forgive sins. When we go to confession, we tell God our sins through the ministry of the priest, express our sorrow for wounding our union with Christ, and resolve to amend our lives. From the mercy of God, we receive absolution from our sins and reconciliation with God, with the family of the Church, and with all whom we have injured. Theologian Romano Guardini writes of the moment of absolution: "Through God's forgiveness, in the eyes of his sacred truth, I am no longer a sinner; in the profoundest depths of my conscience I am no longer guilty. That is what I wanted! It can be; that is the sense of Christ's message."[35]

For Reflection

1. When was your last confession? If it has been a year or more, why have you let this opportunity pass by?
2. What would you tell a person who says, "I don't feel the need to go to a priest and confess. I can confess directly to God"?
3. Why is it said that the First Commandment is the clue for interpreting the other nine?

Prayer

Act of Contrition

O my God, I am heartily sorry for having offended you, and I detest all my sins because I dread the loss of heaven and the pains of hell; but most of all because they offend you, my God, who are all good and deserving of all my love. I firmly resolve, with the help of your grace, to confess my sins, to do penance, and to amend my life. Amen.

CHAPTER TWENTY-TWO

THE SICK AMONG US

Are any among you sick? They should call for the elders of the church and have them pray over them, anointing them with oil in the name of the Lord. The prayer of faith will save the sick, and the Lord will raise them up; and anyone who has committed sins will be forgiven. — JAMES 5:14-15

The Gospels report a number of incidents that illustrate Jesus' compassion for the sick. "He had compassion for them and cured their sick" (Matthew 14:14). The crowds often followed Jesus, sometimes even pushing closely against him.

In the fifth chapter of Mark's Gospel, we read about a woman in a certain crowd who had suffered bleeding outside her menstrual period for twelve years. This ailment not only caused her physical exhaustion but also rendered her ritually unclean (see Leviticus 15:25). She had all the problems of pain along with the religious and social isolation caused by the illness. She had tried many doctors and used up all her savings. No doctor helped her. Desperate, she reached out and touched the hem of Christ's robe. What did she have to lose?

Her plan worked. She felt the flow of blood dry up immediately. At the same time, Jesus noticed that healing power had flowed from him. He stopped and asked who had touched him. The apostles were puzzled because dozens of people were pressing around him. Jesus asked the question because he wanted people to understand that it was the faith of the woman that opened her to a cure, not the magic-like touching of his robe.

The poor woman was terrified. She feared she had offended Jesus and that the miracle would be withdrawn. Shaking with fear she came forward, knelt before him, and told him the truth. Jesus smiled, lifted her up, and looked at her with warmth and compassion. He told her, loud enough for all to hear, that it was her faith that cured her. Affectionately calling her "daughter," he bade her to go in peace and said that she would be free of her illness. Significantly, Jesus also said: "Your faith has saved you" (Mark 5:34, NAB). She had received from Jesus salvation as well as physical healing.

The Christian Meaning of Suffering

"Man can put this question of suffering to God with all the emotion of his heart and with his mind full of dismay and anxiety. God expects the question and listens to it....

"Almost always the individual enters suffering with a *typically human protest and with the question 'why.'* ... He often puts this question to God, and to Christ. Furthermore, he cannot help noticing that the one to whom he puts the question is himself suffering and wishes *to answer him* from the Cross, *from the heart of his own suffering.* Nevertheless, it often takes time, even a long time, for this answer to begin to be interiorly perceived. For Christ does not answer directly and he does not answer in the abstract this human questioning about the meaning of suffering.

Continued on next page

Throughout his ministry, Jesus displayed a loving concern for the bodily and spiritual needs of the sick and expected his followers to do the same. "Cure the sick ... cleanse the lepers.... I was sick and you took care of me" (Matthew 10:8; 25:36).

Continued from previous page

Man hears Christ's saving answer as he himself gradually becomes a sharer in the sufferings of Christ....

"Christ does not explain in the abstract the reasons for suffering, but before all else he says: 'Follow me!' Come! Take part through your suffering in this work of saving the world, a salvation achieved through my suffering! Through my Cross. Gradually, *as the individual takes up his cross,* spiritually uniting himself to the Cross of Christ, the salvific meaning of suffering is revealed before him. He does not discover this meaning at his own human level, but at the level of the suffering of Christ....

"This is not all: the Divine Redeemer wishes to penetrate the soul of every sufferer through the heart of his holy Mother, the first and the most exalted of all the redeemed. As though by a continuation of that motherhood which by the power of the Holy Spirit had given him life, the dying Christ conferred upon the ever Virgin Mary a *new kind of motherhood* — spiritual and universal — towards all human beings, so that every individual, during the pilgrimage of faith, might remain, together with her, closely united to him unto the Cross, and so that every form of suffering, given fresh life by the power of this Cross, should become no longer the weakness of man but the power of God."[36]

— POPE JOHN PAUL II

In a special way, the Church continues Christ's healing work through the Sacrament of Anointing. The faithful should be encouraged to ask for the anointing and receive it with faith and devotion. Anyone who is in danger of death from sickness or old age may receive the sacrament. Those who recover and then have another serious illness may receive the sacrament again. A sick person may be anointed before surgery when a serious illness is the reason for the operation. Elderly people may be anointed, even though no serious illness is present. All those who care for the sick should be taught the meaning and purpose of the sacrament.[37]

For those who are nearing death and on their final journey toward the next life, the Sacrament of the Anointing of the Sick is an anointing unto glory, a sacrament of departure. Baptism began to conform them to the death and resurrection of Christ. This sacrament accompanies the final journey. The sick may also receive a final Eucharist, which we call *viaticum*. It means that Christ is with us "on the way."

Only bishops and priests may confer this sacrament. The celebration consists essentially in anointing the forehead and hands of the sick person (in the Latin rite) as well as other parts of the body (in the Eastern rites). The anointing is accompanied by this prayer in the Latin rite (*Pastoral Care of the Sick*, 25):

> Through this holy anointing
> may the Lord in his love and mercy help you
> with the grace of the Holy Spirit.
>
> May the Lord who frees you from sin
> save you and raise you up.

> "Those who are seriously ill need the special help of God's grace in this time of anxiety, lest they be broken in spirit and, under the pressure of temptation, perhaps weakened in their faith. This is why, through the sacrament of anointing, Christ strengthens the faithful who are afflicted by illness, providing them with the strongest means of support."
>
> — *PASTORAL CARE OF THE SICK*, 5

From apostolic times to the present, the members of the Church have cared for the sick and dying in a variety of ways. Despite the fragmentation of family life and the loss of the extended family due to economic and social changes, there are still caregivers in families looking after an ailing parent, spouse, or child.

In almost every city, where there is a significant Catholic population, a Catholic hospital founded and sponsored by a religious congregation of nuns or brothers still operates, although the latter's presence is vastly reduced through membership decline. Catholic doctors and nurses are called to view their professional status in the light of their faith that joins them to Christ's healing ministry. Church-sponsored hospice care is yet another expression of our concern for the spiritual, mental, emotional, and physical care of the sick. Blessed Mother Teresa's unique ministry to the poorest of the poor — the abandoned dying in the streets of Calcutta and elsewhere — is an inspiring application of Christ's call to care for the sick.

For Reflection

1. What experience have you had of the Sacrament of Anointing?
2. If you received the anointing and were granted a cure for your illness, what impact would that have on your faith?
3. As you read Pope John Paul II's words on the Christian meaning of human suffering, what new light does this shed on your own view of the role of pain in your life?

Prayer

Lord Jesus, healer of our minds, bodies, souls, and emotions, we are grateful for the Sacrament of Anointing. We realize there will be times when we will need the anointing both for our spiritual and physical health. We ask for the graces we need for lifelong conversion. Remind us to be compassionate friends to the sick. May our hearts be homes for faith, hope, and love. Amen.

CHAPTER TWENTY-THREE

THE ORDER OF MELCHIZEDEK

> For it is attested of him,
>   "You are a priest forever,
>   according to the order of Melchizedek."
> — HEBREWS 7:17

When Jesus chose the twelve apostles, he trained them to be his special disciples. He groomed them to be the priests of the new covenant. He revealed to them God's loving plan to save us. They saw how he called his listeners to faith through parables, metaphors, proverbs, the Sermon on the Mount, and the challenge to lose the self, take up the cross, and follow him. They witnessed him using dialogues, debates, and table talk as the means of getting the message across. This was Christ's ministry of the Word and one of the ways he trained his future priests.

Jesus also showed them the need to put his words into action. Christ's deeds were the pastoral context of his words. Today, good and faithful priests still understand the importance of both words and deeds.

The first words Cardinal Joseph Bernardin (1928-1996) spoke to the priests of Chicago as their new leader set the tone of his relationship with them, "I am your brother Joseph." His journey in the priesthood had rocky moments. In his previous post, he served as archbishop of Cincinnati. While there, he belonged to a support group of priests. One day they confronted him about his lifestyle. They noted he was gaining too much weight and that he seemed too ambitious. In their eyes, he appeared too eager to move up the ecclesiastical ladder to a more prestigious rank. Finally, they wondered how serious he was about his prayer life.

To his credit, Bernardin listened to them and resolved to lose weight, temper his ambitions, and pray more. From then on, he rose every morning an hour earlier and devoted himself to prayer. As time moved on, he feared three things. He feared he would be falsely accused of sexual abuse. He dreaded the possibility of having cancer. He worried that he would die before his mother and not be able to care for her. All three fears came true.

A former seminarian said that he had been abused by Bernardin. The cardinal immediately called a press conference and denied the allegation. He asked for a thorough investigation. As it turned out, the accuser recanted his accusation. And when the young man lay dying of AIDS, Bernardin went to visit him, forgave him for what he had done, and anointed him.

Eventually, the cardinal contracted a painful pancreatic cancer. At the hospital, he refused to use the VIP entrance and went instead to the general waiting room, where he made friends with fellow sufferers and ministered to them. He wrote to the Supreme Court and begged them not to approve physician-assisted suicide: "As one who is dying I have come to appreciate much more the gift of life." He wrote a letter to all of the bishops, asking for their prayers to help him get through this challenge. Lastly, he sent out his Christmas cards. His longtime aide and friend, Monsignor Kenneth Velo, preached the homily at the funeral, using the theme from the road to Emmaus:

"Didn't he teach us. Didn't he show us the way?" All Chicago mourned, along with the cardinal's grieving mother. On that freezing day, November 14, 1996, people knelt in the streets as the hearse bearing his body passed by.

A Way of Life

"I can't imagine being anything but a priest. Just think, I consider lack of imagination to be a crime and yet I haven't the imagination not to be a priest. For me, being a priest isn't just a choice; it's a way of life. It's what water is for a fish, the sky for a bird. I really believe in Christ. Jesus for me is not an abstract idea — he's a personal friend.

"Being a priest has never disappointed me nor given me regrets. Celibacy, chastity, the absence of a family in the way that laymen understand it, all this has never been a burden to me. If I've missed certain joys, I have others more sublime. If you only know what I feel when I say Mass, how I become one with it! The Mass for me is truly Calvary, and the Resurrection: it's a mad joy!

"Look, there are those born to sing, those born to write, those born to play soccer, and those who are born to be priests. I started saying so at the age of 8 and certainly not because my parents put the idea in my head. My father was a Mason, and my mother went to Church once a year. I even remember my father got frightened and one day said to me: 'My son, you are always saying you want to be a priest. Do you know what that means? A priest is someone who doesn't belong to himself, because he belongs to God and to his people?' I know. That's why I want to be a priest."[38]

— Archbishop Hélder Câmara, famed for his love for the poor in Brazil

Joseph Bernardin showed us what a dedicated priest can be like.

How did the first priests — the apostles — learn to be priests? What was their priestly formation? Clearly, Jesus' miracles of compassion illustrated his commands to love others as they loved themselves. They received hints of his divinity when he walked on water and provided a wine miracle at Cana and a bread miracle on the mountain. But his pastoral acts really won their hearts: saving the life of the woman in adultery, converting the Samaritan woman and the little man in the sycamore tree, impressing them with his remarkable prayer, forgiving his persecutors and Peter, converting Thomas, and many other forms of Good Shepherd examples.

Jesus' words gave meaning to his deeds. His deeds showed the meaning of his words. Both elements formed the apostles as priests and as pastors. At the Last Supper, it all came together. After instituting the Eucharist and giving them the bread that became his Body and the wine that became his Blood, he said: "Do this in memory of me." Pope John Paul II explains this command in the following way:

> When he says to the Apostles, "Do this in memory of me" he constitutes the ministers of this sacrament in the Church, in which for all time the sacrifice offered by him for the redemption of the world must be continued.... He commands these same ministers to act by virtue of their sacramental priesthood in his place: "*in persona Christi*." Holy Thursday is every year the day of the birth of the Eucharist and the birthday of our priesthood.[39]

> "Young people ask me what it takes to be a priest. I tell them: You need two things, a funny bone and a backbone. If you don't have a sense of humor, you won't be able to preach the Good News. You also need a backbone; if you don't, you will soon fall in line with the surrounding culture."[40]
>
> — FATHER ARNOLD WEBER, O.S.B.

St. Peter addressed all baptized Christians in these words: "You are a chosen race, a royal priesthood, a holy nation, God's own people, in order that you may proclaim the mighty acts of him who called you out of darkness into his marvelous light" (1 Peter 2:9). Through the Sacrament of Baptism, all Christians share in the priesthood of Christ. This is known as the "common priesthood of the faithful." Through Holy Orders, there is a different participation in Christ's priesthood — that of bishop, priest, and deacon. Bishops receive the fullness of Holy Orders and are the chief teachers, sanctifiers, and shepherds of their dioceses. Priests are united with the bishops in dignity and are called to be the co-workers with them. Deacons receive Holy Orders but not the ministerial priesthood. Deacons are ordained to baptize, proclaim the Gospel, preach the homily, assist the bishop or priest in celebrating the Eucharist, assist at and bless marriages, and preside at funerals.

The ordained priesthood and the common priesthood of the faithful complement each other while remaining essentially different. The common priesthood is devoted to a life of faith, hope, and love in the Holy Spirit. The ministerial priesthood serves the common priesthood's quest for holiness, especially by celebrating the Eucharist, hearing confessions, preaching God's Word, and serving God's people in many other ways. St. Augustine expressed this in his axiom, "With you, I am a Christian. For you, I am a bishop."

For Reflection

1. What are your expectations of bishops, priests, and deacons?
2. What must be done to increase the number of vocations to the priesthood?
3. If the Eucharist is the summit and source of Christian life, why is there not a greater surge to join the priesthood?

Prayer

Christ, our high priest, we need good pastors to be stewards of God's mysteries and doctors for our souls. We ask you to awaken the call to priesthood in a whole new generation. We pray for our bishops and priests, that they may always be led by the Holy Spirit, filled with compassion, and enthusiastic about their calling. Amen.

CHAPTER TWENTY-FOUR

TWO IN ONE FLESH

> *The vocation to marriage is written in the very nature of man and woman as they came from the hand of the Creator. Marriage is not a purely human institution despite the many variations it may have undergone through the centuries in different cultures, social structures, and spiritual attitudes.*
> — CCC, 1603

Marriage has always been part of God's plan for his children. Over a five-year period at the beginning of his pontificate, Pope John Paul II devoted his Wednesday audiences to a unique interpretation of Genesis 1-3. He describes the beginning of Adam's life as an experience of original solitude. Once created, Adam finds himself alone in the garden. Human life begins in solitude. Adam's solitude is a condition that enables him to focus on God alone. He is the only one on earth able to walk and talk with God. We can carry that original solitude in our hearts when we stand before God and rejoice in his presence.

But Adam is different from all the animals. The animal kingdom is not a substitute for human companionship. As God says, "It is not good that the man should be alone; I will make him a helper as his partner" (Genesis 2:18). Then God casts Adam into a deep sleep and takes a rib from Adam's side and creates a woman from the rib. When God brings the woman to the man, he exclaims with grateful joy: "This at last is bone of my bones and flesh of my flesh" (Genesis 2:23). Scripture goes on to explain, "Therefore a man leaves his father and mother and clings to his wife, and they become one flesh"(Genesis 2:24).

Eve has a different body, but she is clearly a human person like Adam. The two of them complement each other. Both of them are images of God, who looks at them and declares this new creation is very good! In this scene, God reveals the original unity of man and woman, who were created to relate to God and to each other. God is a communion of three Persons, yet an absolute unity. Adam and Eve are two persons, but destined to be united in one flesh. Their union of love is meant to reflect the communion of love in the Trinity. God blesses the couple and tells them the meaning of his blessing: "Be fruitful and multiply" (Genesis 1:28).

In his talks, the pope unfolded yet one more insight about this couple — namely, that they were naked but unashamed, an experience the pope calls "original nakedness." Their bodies did not stimulate lust, but rather symbolized their freedom to love each other in a manner God intended for their marriage and all marriages.

Fresh from the hand of God there was no barrier to their communion with each other and no difficulties in forming a relationship that united them to each other. Original nakedness placed sex in the context of relationship. Their bodies were more relational than sexual. At the dawn of creation, the first couple understood their calling to love and responsibility. Their freedom meant the capacity to choose only the good.

Sadly, this beautiful original relationship was spoiled by original sin. In subsequent centuries, as chronicled in the Old Testament, people struggled to recover the basic meaning of marriage as outlined in Genesis. Though Moses per-

Creative Crayons

At each wedding one of my students, Father George P. O'Neill, performs, he likes to give the bride and groom a box of crayons, along with the following instructions:

> First, I give you the brown crayon. Brown is the color of the earth, from which God created you and to which one day you will return. Today God calls you to build a home on this earth. Be sure it is on rock and not sand.
>
> I give you this green crayon because green is the color of hope. I encourage you to take every dream you have for your marriage and go for it.
>
> Now here is a blue crayon for those days of conflict when you need to say, "I'm sorry. I love you today more than ever before." Be quick to forgive. Be even faster to accept forgiveness. Nothing kills a marriage more than holding grudges and bad feelings.
>
> Next I have a yellow crayon for you just to remind you of this wonderful day God gives you for your marriage. Think of this day when you need to put a smile back on your face and cheer in your heart.
>
> I give you this orange crayon that catches the mellow rays of the sunset. Don't grow old too fast. Never let your love become stale with the passing of the years. Stay young in love. Dance together. Play together. Sing together. Stay close to the dream that brought you together.
>
> Here's a purple crayon, a royal color to remind you that soon you will not just be another man and

Continued on next page

Continued from previous page

woman. God calls you to be husband and wife, the world's most honored union. With it comes the wonderful responsibility to care for each other. Handle each other's hearts carefully. A heart is easily broken.

Finally, a red crayon. It is the color of the Holy Spirit. The Spirit brought you together and to this altar. Make yours a holy marriage with prayer, worship, fidelity, and growth in virtues with the graces of the Holy Spirit.

These crayons are no good if kept in a box. Love is useless if locked in your heart. Take out the love and give it to each other. Do it every hour of every day until God calls you home.

mitted divorce due to the pressure of people, the Books of Tobit and Ruth witness God's plan for marriage, describing the fidelity to marital vows and the tenderness of love that should exist between husband and wife.

Jesus' teaching again reminds us of the divine plan for marriage. In a discussion about divorce, Jesus reminded his listeners how God created marriage. Man and woman became two in one flesh: "What God has joined together, let no one separate" (Matthew 19:6). St. Paul reinforced Christ's teaching on marriage: "The wife should not separate from her husband ... and ... the husband should not divorce his wife" (1 Corinthians 7:10-11). At the marriage feast of Cana, Jesus performed his first miracle. As the *Catechism* says, "The Church attaches great importance to Jesus' presence at the wedding at Cana. She

The Rites of Matrimony

"According to the Latin tradition, the spouses as ministers of Christ's grace mutually confer upon each other the sacrament of Matrimony by expressing their consent before the Church. In the traditions of the Eastern Churches, the priests (bishops or presbyters) are witnesses to the mutual consent given by the spouses (cf. CCEO, can. 817), but for the validity of the sacrament their blessing is also necessary (cf. CCEO, can. 828)" (CCC, 1623).

The free consent of the couple is at the heart of the celebration, given in the presence of the Church's minister, two witnesses, and the congregation. The priest invites their consent by saying, "Since it is your intention to enter into marriage, join your right hands, and declare your consent before God and his Church" (*Rite of Marriage*, 25). The consent is also symbolized by the blessing and exchange of rings, with the words: "[T]ake this ring as a sign of my love and fidelity. In the name of the Father, and of the Son, and of the Holy Spirit" (*Rite of Marriage*, 28).

Generally, marriage ceremonies take place in the context of the Mass, where the spouses' communion with each other receives the ultimate blessing in taking their Eucharistic Lord into their hearts.

sees in it the confirmation of the goodness of marriage and the proclamation that thenceforth marriage will be an efficacious sign of Christ's presence" (CCC, 1613).

When following God's plan for marriage, partners experience three particular blessings:

- The first blessing is the permanent and unbreakable bond of love between the spouses. They are called to form one mind, heart, soul, and body with each other. These natural virtues are elevated by the Sacrament of Marriage to the expression of Christian ideals. Their permanent bond is strengthened by the presence of the third partner to their union, Jesus Christ, who perfects their profound love for each other.

- The second blessing of marriage, which the sacrament protects, is their marital fidelity to each other. Their union is more than a legal contract; it is a covenant, a deeply personal commitment that draws its ability to work from the power of Christ's own unassailable fidelity to the Church. Marital love is a lifetime, not just "until further notice."

- The third blessing of marriage is openness to children and their spiritual, moral, educational, physical, and emotional welfare.

For Reflection

1. When you look at successful marriages, what is it that makes them work?
2. Why is it essential to be open to the possibility of children? What are the gifts that children bring to a marriage?
3. Why is living together before marriage destructive for marital fidelity and stability?

Prable

Prayer

We thank you, O God, for the love you have implanted in our hearts. May it always inspire us to be kind in our words, considerate of feeling, and concerned for each other's needs and wishes. Help us to be understanding and forgiving of human weaknesses and failings. Increase our faith and trust in you, and may your prudence guide our life and love. Bless our marriage, O God, with peace and happiness, and make our love fruitful for your glory and our joy, both here and in eternity.[41]

SECTION THREE

SATISFYING YOUR HUNGER FOR GOD

CHAPTER TWENTY-FIVE

MORALITY AND VIRTUE

> *Finally, beloved, whatever is true, whatever is honorable, whatever is just, whatever is pure, whatever is pleasing, whatever is commendable, if there is any excellence and if there is anything worthy of praise, think about these things.* — PHILIPPIANS 4:8

Catholic moral teaching includes both a covenant of love with God and commandments and rules that help us express the practical meaning of covenant love. On Mount Sinai, God first concluded a covenant union with Moses and only then gave him the Ten Commandments (see Exodus 19:3-6). Christ's Sermon on the Mount began with the covenant language of the Eight Beatitudes, in which he held up eight ways to happiness, thus making joy the goal and motivation of morality. Only after that came practical ways (i.e., rules) for living the beatitudes — for rules without love are harsh; love without rules is vague.

> "How is it then that I seek you, Lord? Since in seeking you, my God, I seek a happy life, let me seek you so that my soul may live, for my body draws life from my soul and my soul draws life from you."
>
> — ST. AUGUSTINE

The moral life also requires the responsible use of our freedom. God gave us the power of reason so that we are free to control our behavior in the light of God's truths. We are not robots, forced to live by outward pressures on inward compulsions. Normally, we are basically free to act morally. Yet our responsibility for an act can be lessened by ignorance, fear, and other emotional factors.

The more we choose to do what is good, the greater will be our feeling of inner freedom. On the other hand, the more we decide to do what is evil, the greater will be our loss of freedom, because sin is a ruthless master bent on enslaving us. Freedom never means the right to say or do whatever we want, but rather whatever we should say and do in accordance with truth and the will of God. People who are truly free in this sense have the best chance for happiness. The evil one tries to persuade us that rules and commandments take the joy out of life. That is only true if they are separated from the love of God and neighbor and the real truth about freedom.

All great cultures began with people who knew the importance of practicing virtues in order to have the inner strength to build a new society. World religions knew the same secret. A rule of life required the discipline that served the life of virtues. Christianity has always prized the virtues that make the moral life accessible and give it the teeth to hold on when severe tests arise. It is no mistake that the word "virtue" comes from Latin roots that speak of power and energy. People of every age of history and culture have known that virtues are habits of mind and heart that help us govern our behavior and control our passions.

What, then, are some of these virtues that we need to incorporate into our lives? They include self-discipline, a work ethic and a sense of responsibility, reliability, honesty, courage, perseverance, and loyalty. Traditionally, we group them around the cardinal virtues of prudence, justice, temperance, and fortitude.

How do we acquire these virtues? Stories of virtuous people inspire us and give us the belief that living virtuously is possible. Their good example will motivate us to imitate what we encounter.

One historical example of a man who lived according to virtue is St. Thomas Becket (1118-1170). Bright and charming, good at hunting and the military ways of knights, Thomas attracted the attention of the archbishop of Canterbury. At 25, he became a deacon and was sent to study law in France, a project that involved research in Bologna and Rome. Impressed with Becket's unusual talents, especially his political skills, King Henry II appointed him chancellor. For the next seven years, Becket and Henry enjoyed a warm relationship. As an ultimate insider, Becket learned the ways of secular power, but as a cleric he also saw the legitimate demands of the Church.

When Henry decided to make him archbishop of Canterbury, thinking that Becket would be his pawn in controlling the Church, he paid no attention to Becket's protests that this would not work. Pressure from the king and from a number of influential bishops prevailed on Becket to accept the post. Gradually, the conflicts that Becket foresaw emerged, especially on issues of protecting Church property as well as trial of clergy in Church courts rather than secular ones. The tensions grew fierce, and the situation clearly illustrated the difficulties of applying Christ's teaching about Church and state: "Render to Caesar the things that are Caesar's, and to God the things that are God's" (Mark 12:17, RSV). For Becket, this was not just a legal quarrel; it was a moral one in which the king was interfering in the life of the Church.

Becket went into exile for six years until he believed it was safe to return. It was too late. In a fit of frustration, the king asked: "Who will rid me of this troublesome priest?" Several barons interpreted this as permission to murder Becket. On December 29, 1170, the barons entered Canterbury Cathedral, interrupted Evening Prayer, and with swords and an axe killed Becket. His death shocked all of Europe. Henry was compelled to do penance by being scourged at the martyr's tomb, which then became one of the most popular pilgrimage shrines in Christendom.

Education in the life of the virtues, and in the methods to acquire such good habits, can be very effective. Daily practice of the virtues, doing them over and over again until they are grooved into our character and behavior, is an essential step toward the life of virtue. Repetition of each virtue in the great variety of life experiences lends excitement to the quest and joy in the achievement.

The Holy Spirit enriches us with the gifts of faith, hope, and charity — the theological virtues. These basic supernatural virtues help us negotiate our relationship with God and others from a divine perspective. They also infuse a spiritual energy into the practice of the natural, or cardinal, virtues mentioned above.

Our life of faith begins at our baptism, but it demands a lifetime of growth in order to affect our many stages of human development. Unless this happens, faith remains stunted, even childish, and therefore easy to lose when adult complexity is not matched with faith advancement. Hope and love also summon us to lifelong maturing.

Grace and Sin

The context of the moral life is the grand drama of the power of life facing down the power of death. The framework of morality is the divine adventure of the entrance of the Son of God into history to correct the tragedy of the sin of Adam and Eve by bringing us salvation and the life of grace that transforms us into Christ. The situation of every human being is a battle between good and evil, a confrontation in each life that only concludes when the curtain of death falls and is followed by judgment in the next life. This invisible war of good and evil seems unseen in one sense due to a secularized culture that distracts us from the true "reality show" that hovers over and within every person.

Christ won the war by conquering sin on Calvary and death at the Resurrection. However, the battle of good and evil continues in the life of every human being and in every generation. Christ's victory over sin and evil is available to us and gives us the confidence that the war we feel in our souls can be won by the graces of Christ.

We do not grow in these virtues without a strong relationship with the Holy Spirit. They are powers of the supernatural that seek to penetrate our natural life in a supportive and dynamic manner. Faith, hope, and love are the trinity of virtues that assure us of life with the Trinity on earth and prepare us for eternal life hereafter. These virtues have a bonus whereby they make our human virtues more dynamic and increase their stability and effectiveness in our lives.

For Reflection

1. What virtues have you found most difficult to practice?
2. How would you convince people that freedom is the ability to choose what you should and not just what you please?
3. What would you say to someone who believes that moral laws make us unhappy by restricting us? How would you convince them that these laws are the road to lasting joy and righteous freedom?

Prayer

Almighty God, stand with us in the battle between life and death that seems so overwhelming. Strengthen our virtues so that we enter the conflict with your grace that conquers sin. Give us the confidence we need to believe in Christ's victory over sin and death. Amen.

CHAPTER TWENTY-SIX

"HE ALONE IS MY ROCK AND MY SALVATION"

> *"You shall love the Lord your God with all your heart, and with all your soul, and with all your mind, and with all your strength."* — MARK 12:30

The most important of the Ten Commandments is the first one. Without faith in God, the other commandments, valuable as they are, lose the energy they demand of us. Lacking a loving relationship with the living God, we will regard the rules that follow as optional, even if reasonably convincing. Robbed of the dynamism of knowing and loving God, we can become detached from the nine other rules that show us how to deepen our relationship with God.

Belief in God is more than an abstract idea. Yes, faith is belief in a creed and in doctrines about God, but it is far more than that. Christian faith is, first of all, a commitment to a real being, a God who is a loving unity of Father, Son, and Spirit. Our faith is inclusive, focused on Christ, who reveals the full picture of God as a trinity of Persons who love each of us with an eternal affection. The centuries of encounter with the living God in history, in the Church, and in the bloodstream of our family traditions emphasize a devotion to God that resonates with the complicated links we experience among us as parents, children, sisters, brothers, cousins, and so on.

Conversion — The Search for God

Conversion to faith in God can be an experience either of our search for God or of God's search for us. C. S. Lewis (1898-1963) claimed that it was God who entered his young adult life when he lived as an atheist. He said the conversion was due to being "surprised by joy."

Lewis was born into an Irish Protestant family in Belfast. His mother died when he was 10, leaving him with a loneliness that prevailed through his adolescence, when he formally gave up his faith in God. He studied at Oxford University and was invited to be a professor there after his graduation.

Gradually, he was faced with a number of challenges to his position about the nonexistence of God. He was surprised to find out that a number of his closest friends believed in God and were active Christians. They talked with him freely about Christianity and Christ, and they witnessed their faith in God and in Christ as the Son of God. Among them was a Catholic, J. R. R. Tolkien, whose *Lord of the Rings* has become a literary classic. Lewis argued with his friends that he really did not want to find God, but God sought Lewis and found him. Like Jonah in the Bible who ran from God, Lewis fled what the poet Francis Thompson called the "Hound of Heaven."

The first milestone in his conversion was totally unexpected. Lewis says it occurred one day in 1929 when he happened to take a bus ride. When he boarded the bus, he was an atheist. When he got off the bus, he found himself believing in God.

His next turn to God was like St. Paul's Damascus conversion. In 1931, his brother Warren drove him to

Continued on next page

Continued from previous page

the zoo. Lewis wrote, "When I set out, I did not believe Christ was the Son of God and when we reached the zoo I did. It was like when a man, after a long sleep, still lying motionless in bed, becomes aware that he is now awake."

Lewis joined the Anglican Church, and for the next thirty years he became an eloquent speaker and writer about Christ and the Christian faith. He became a disciple of Christ who made countless disciples. His World War II radio talks on the BBC uplifted both the spirits of the British people and their faith; these talks were published in his most widely read book, *Mere Christianity.*

When we speak of the family as a domestic Church, we affirm that the Christian home is a laboratory of the ways we love, breathe, and worship a God who loves us even more. So belief in God is much more than a faith statement. It is a declaration of love of the soul of our being: an almighty Father, a saving Son, and a sanctifying Spirit — divine Persons who are woven into our family circle as our origin and destiny.

In his discussions with the religious leaders of his time, Christ is asked several times, "What is the greatest commandment?" He replies that the greatest commandment has two aspects. The first is the call to love God with all our mind, heart, and strength. Essentially connected to loving God is the command to love our neighbor as ourselves.

Most polls of American religion report that practically everybody claims to believe in God. Probing this survey more closely we may find a different answer.

Suppose the question is, "Do you love God — and if so, what does that mean?" Some may reply it means keeping the commandments by not lying or stealing. Others might connect it with helping others. Another group could tell us it's about caring for the poor. Yet a number of people have been known to reply that it refers to self-fulfillment. It is instructive to note that most atheists and secularists agree with these practices.

"You must picture me alone in that room in Magdalen, night after night, feeling, whenever my mind lifted for even a second from my work, the steady, unrelenting approach of Him whom I desired earnestly not to meet. That which I had greatly feared had at last come upon me. In the Trinity term of 1929 I gave in, and admitted that God was God, and knelt and prayed: perhaps that night the most dejected and reluctant convert in all England. But who can duly adore that Love which will open the high gates to a prodigal who is brought in, kicking, struggling, resentful, and darting his eyes in every direction for a chance to escape."[42]

— C. S. LEWIS

Probably all Catholics would follow the above practices, yet well over half of all registered Catholics rarely participate in Sunday liturgy. Even some of the ones who do show up and go to Communion may have only a shallow link with God. For all too many Christians, deeds, not creeds or divine-human relationships, are what it is all

False Gods

"For all that is in the world, the lust of the flesh and the lust of the eyes and the pride of life, is not of the Father but is of the world" (1 John 2:16, RSV). This teaching of St. John sums up what happens to us when we abandon faith in the real God.

We are all born with infinite longings, and when we deny God we create false deities. Generally speaking, there are three false gods:

♦ The first is born when we make a god of our own bodies. Sexual pleasure is elevated to be the supreme value sought. This is one of history's oldest idols, some instances of which are found in Scripture as well as in examples of temple prostitution in Greek and Roman culture.

♦ Another route to idolatry is making a god of our minds. Such people worship their education and intelligence, claiming there is no knowledge beyond what reason can know and no moral law beyond what they choose to be right. This god is known as pride, which nurtures our overblown egos. It is an excessive form of worshiping the self.

♦ The third typical false god is greed or the love of money. "The love of money is the root of all evils; it is through this craving that some have wandered away from the faith" (1 Timothy 6:10, RSV). When people lose the value of the spiritual, they resort to the worship of the material world. The axiom of this idolatry is "I am what I have."

♦ In each of these cases, we abandon the real God and create god substitutes. Instead of faith in the infinite

Continued on next page

Continued from previous page

love of God, we settle for infinitely less. We are dimin-
ished. We acquire eyes that do not see with faith. We
have mouths that cannot speak truth. We have feet
that cannot walk in love. We have become shadows
who are satisfied with the lies we tell ourselves. It is a
lonely life whose artificial goals need to be stimulated
by more erotica, more knowledge, or more money.

about. Both practicing and nonpracticing Catholics face
the challenge of loving God directly and growing more
deeply in a lifelong, interpersonal union with God.

Loving God does require a result in good works. But
first, loving God means we actually are in touch with our
blessed Lord every day. Why else does the Second Commandment stress God's call to a holy life and the Third
Commandment insist on the primacy of worship in our
lives? The true test of loving a person is attention and
time. If we rarely pay attention to God or spend quality
time on a consistent basis with our Lord, what does such
love mean?

For Reflection

1. In what ways do you express your faith in God in doctrine and celebrate it in liturgy?
2. What false gods might be present in your life?
3. How would you reply to people who tell you that deeds,
not creeds, are what are really important?

───────

Prayer

My soul finds rest in God alone;
    my salvation comes from him.
He alone is my rock and my salvation;
    he is my fortress, I will never be shaken….
Find rest, O my soul, in God alone;
    my hope comes from him.
He alone is my rock and my salvation;
    he is my fortress, I will not be shaken.

— PSALM 62:1-2, 5-6, NIV

CHAPTER TWENTY-SEVEN

HOLY BE HIS NAME

> *One shows respect for the holy Name of God by blessing it, praising it and glorifying it.* — COMPENDIUM, 447

On his twenty-first birthday, the prophet Isaiah received an invitation to the Temple for the enthronement of Jotham as the new king (Isaiah 6). Amid the splendor of music, incense, and royal processions, Isaiah had a profound and mystical vision of God's glory. He heard angels sing about the holiness and glory of God. God's robe seemed to fill the Temple, giving Isaiah the feeling of intimacy with the Lord. Then the foundations of the Temple trembled and clouds of smoke shut out the vision.

Now Isaiah stood dazed and alone, and he gradually became aware of himself in contrast to what he had seen. He compared his weak and sinful condition to the immense beauty and unimaginable holiness of God. He looked into his heart and made a serious examination of conscience. This impelled him to utter in anguished admission, "Woe is me! I am lost, for I am a man of unclean lips." He proceeded to give the reason for his judgment: "My eyes have seen the King, the LORD of hosts!" (v. 5). The cloud disappeared and the vision returned. An angel took a burning coal and pressed it against the lips of Isaiah, telling him: "Now that this has touched your lips, your guilt has departed and your sin is blotted out" (v. 7). Then God said, "Whom shall I send, and who will go for us?" Isaiah replied, "Here am I; send me!" (v. 8).

God had a mission for the prophet and framed his call as an invitation that was addressed to the freedom of this young man. Cleansed from sin by God, Isaiah had the courage to accept the mission with obedience and love. Isaiah had come to the Temple to witness the enthronement of a king, but was privileged to experience the holiness of God. He walked away from the Temple as a new prophet, one of the greatest who ever lived. For nearly fifty years, he witnessed the glory of God, who willed that people should treat one another with simple justice. His most popular title for God was "the Holy One of Israel."

After the Preface at every Mass, we sing or recite the hymn of the angels based on Isaiah's vision: "Holy, holy, holy ..." (Isaiah 6:3). This focus on the holiness of God reminds all of us that we have a vocation to sanctity, which reflects the meaning of the Second Commandment: "You shall not take the name of the LORD your God in vain" (cf. Deuteronomy 5:11).

Profanity and blasphemy once sent underground by the courtesy of an observant public order now has too often raised disrespect for the name of God as accepted speech that numbs the users' consciousness of the self-destructive effect of what they say. Coarse talk desensitizes others to the point that it creates a need for little victories over the once-admired discipline of reverence for the sacred. Simply put, when God is habitually disdained in everyday discourse, what will happen to those who want to have a relationship of awe, trust, affection, and humble love for God? When the clutter of a rainfall of profanities distracts and interrupts us, how can we truly seek the face of God? When blasphemy becomes cool, how long can the heat of a divine passion be sought and nourished?

The Wrong Use of God's Name

In Christian history, we have our own sad record of the wrong use of God's name. When the practice of slavery occurred in our southern states, there were those who justified this in God's name. When the excesses of the Inquisition occurred, advocates sought to defend themselves in God's name. Unjust wars fought by Christian nations were sometimes cloaked with the name of God. Closer to home, family quarrels and grudges often were justified by claiming God was "on our side."

Reciting these sad examples is not meant to make ourselves feel superior to the sinners of ages past, but rather to serve as cautionary tales to restrain such behavior on our part today. As we all know in our more honest moments, the temptation to use God as a cloak for malice can corrupt the best of us when we fail to be utterly honest about our intentions and the purposes that guide our consciences.

Just before he ascended to heaven, Jesus said to the apostles: "You will receive power when the Holy Spirit has come upon you; and you will be my witnesses in Jerusalem, in all Judea and Samaria, and to the ends of the earth" (Acts 1:8). Jesus also addresses these words to each of us. The Holy Spirit fills us with divine power to understand the Church's teachings and the ways to apply them to our lives.

If we are going to respect God's name in a secular culture, we need the courage and boldness that the Holy Spirit will give us. Read the Acts of the Apostles and see how the Spirit transformed those fearful men, huddled timidly behind closed doors, into brave disciples of Christ. He can do the same thing for us today, if we let him.

For Reflection

1. How would you rate the use of language in your family? G, PG, PG-13, R, or X?
2. How can you eliminate profanity from your vocabulary or that of family members?
3. What could your parish do to help promote a greater respect for the name of God?

Prayer

Almighty God — Father, Son, and Holy Spirit — we praise your holy name. In praying your name, we adore your mystery and majesty. In respecting you, we learn to respect one another. In glorifying your name, we acquire a sense of the sacred, which we begin to experience in the midst of this world. As we reverence you and one another here on earth, we pray for the graces needed to discover constantly your holy presence in all creation. Amen.

CHAPTER TWENTY-EIGHT

KEEP HOLY THE SABBATH

> *For in six days the LORD made heaven and earth, the sea, and all that is in them, but rested the seventh day; therefore the LORD blessed the sabbath day and consecrated it.* — EXODUS 20:11

In the Creation story, God worked six days to create the world and its inhabitants and then "rested" on the seventh day, known as the Sabbath. It was God who blessed the Sabbath day and made it holy. The Third Commandment calls us to observe the holiness of this day that God made holy in a special way. Although this commandment originated in the Jewish covenant, it prepares for the Sunday of the new and eternal covenant. Our Sunday is meant to be an exalted occasion of our loving relationship with God.

Every Sunday is a day to refer all things back to God. In the Sunday Mass, we celebrate the resurrection of the Son of God, who offers us endless divine life and love; and we gather around the altar to join the angels in singing praises to God — Father, Son, and Spirit — for the privilege of a relationship that is the most real and rewarding kind of relating possible for any human being. Sunday Mass is a time of re-living the glory of creation and the incredible gift of salvation, of chanting amens to the promises made in our spousal link with God.

For several centuries of Christianity, the people observed Sunday as a day of worship without being able to treat it as a day of rest. Only when the emperor Constantine gave Christians religious freedom and declared Sunday a day of rest did the full meaning of Sunday apply to the public order. Today, regular Sunday Mass attendance among U.S. Catholics has declined to 25 percent in most sections of the country. In many European countries, the percentage is even lower. Besides this, the commercializing of the culture means that many stores remain open on Sundays. With the rise of husbands and wives both engaged in full-time jobs, shopping on weekends becomes a necessity. Pastors complain that various children's sports schedule practices and competitions on Sunday mornings, increasing the difficulty of family participation in worship.

Pope Benedict calls us to reclaim the Sabbath, to keep holy the Day of the World. In his homily at the closing of a Eucharistic Congress, he said:

> The intention of this Eucharistic Congress, which ends today, was once again to present Sunday as the "weekly Easter," an expression of the identity of the Christian community and the center of its life and mission.
>
> The chosen theme —*"Without Sunday we cannot live"* — takes us back to the year 304, when the Emperor Diocletian forbade Christians, on pain of death, from possessing the Scriptures, from gathering on Sundays to celebrate the Eucharist, and from building places in which to hold their assemblies.
>
> In Abitene, a small village in present-day Tunisia, 49 Christians were taken by surprise one Sunday while

they were celebrating the Eucharist, gathered in the house of Octavius Felix, thereby defying the imperial prohibitions. They were arrested and taken to Carthage to be interrogated by the Proconsul Anulinus.

Significant among other things is the answer a certain Emeritus gave to the Proconsul, who asked him why on earth they had disobeyed the Emperor's severe orders. He replied: *"Sine dominico non possumus"*: that is, we cannot live without joining together on Sunday to celebrate the Eucharist. We would lack the strength to face our daily problems and not to succumb.

After atrocious tortures, these 49 martyrs of Abitene were killed. Thus, they confirmed their faith with bloodshed. They died, but they were victorious: today we remember them in the glory of the Risen Christ.

The experience of the martyrs of Abitene is also one on which we 21st-century Christians should reflect. It is not easy for us either to live as Christians.... From a spiritual point of view, the world in which we find ourselves, often marked by unbridled consumerism, religious indifference, and a secularism closed to transcendence, can appear a desert just as *"vast and terrible"* (Deuteronomy 8:15) as the one we heard about in the first reading from the Book of Deuteronomy.[43]

When asked for reasons why they fail to participate in Sunday worship, some Catholics say that they are too busy, or that they don't "get anything out of it," or that there is no moral obligation to attend Mass. At its basis, the loss of Catholic culture may be cited as the main reason for this attitude toward weekly worship. In former times, the Christian culture supported devotion to Sunday worship. In the more fervent places of our nation, the sense of God's presence was palpable, and customs of weekly worship prevailed extensively. There are still parts of our nation where a religious culture is still moderately strong, where Catholicism is actually expanding — but it is not fruitful to dwell on what has been lost. It is always more useful to light a candle than to curse the darkness. There is a greater path to the solution by facing the divine origins of creation and redemption.

"I have been able to celebrate Holy Mass in chapels built along mountain paths, on lakeshores and seacoasts; I have celebrated it on altars built in stadiums and in city squares…. This varied scenario of celebrations of the Eucharist has given me a powerful experience of its universal and, so to speak, cosmic character. Yes, cosmic! Because even when it is celebrated on the humble altar of a country church, the Eucharist is always in some way celebrated *on the altar of the world.* It unites heaven and earth. It embraces and permeates all creation."[44]

— Pope John Paul II

From the beginning, God has revealed his connection with creatures as a loving relationship. God covenants with all of us with a love that never ends. At the dawn of creation, God smiled on us with a nuptial attitude. From God's point of view, there is no emphasis on distance from us or an impersonal chasm between the Creator and the created. God the Tremendous Lover put that stamp on his beloved creation from very beginning. The prophet Hosea wrote a marvelous passage about this:

> "I will make for you a covenant on that day with the beasts of the field, the birds of the air, and the creeping things of the ground; and I will abolish the bow, the sword, and war from the land; and I will make you lie down in safety. And I will espouse you for ever; I will espouse you in righteousness and in justice, in steadfast love, and in mercy. I will espouse you in faithfulness; and you shall know the LORD." (Hosea 2:18-20, RSV)

In his first major appearance to his apostles, the Risen Lord came to them on that Easter night, dynamically filled with life and rich with the messianic gift of peace. Earlier that day, he had also appeared and walked with two disciples on the road to Emmaus. He taught them from Scripture that he was supposed to suffer and so enter his glory. He sat with them at Emmaus and revealed his risen glory to them in the breaking of the bread. This vivid link between Easter and the Eucharist is the salient reality of every Sunday Mass. Christ's gestures and blessing of the bread recall the Last Supper and allude to the name for the Eucharist — the "breaking of the bread," as it was called by the first generation of Christians.

As Pope John Paul II writes in his splendid apostolic letter *Dies Domini* (On Keeping the Lord's Day):

> In every Eucharistic celebration, the Risen Lord is encountered in the Sunday assembly at the twofold

table of the word and of the Bread of Life. The table of the word offers the same understanding of the history of salvation and especially of the Paschal Mystery which the Risen Jesus himself gave to his disciples: it is Christ who speaks, present as he is in his word "when Sacred Scripture is read in the Church" (*Sacrosanctum Concilium* [Constitution on the Sacred Liturgy], 7; cf. 33). At the table of the Bread of Life, the Risen Lord becomes really, substantially and enduringly present through the memorial of his Passion and Resurrection, and the Bread of Life is offered as a pledge of future glory.[45]

For Reflection

1. If you wanted to persuade some inactive Catholics to return to weekly Sunday Mass, what are some approaches you would try?
2. What thoughts do you have about the improvement of the homilies at Mass?
3. Why is it generally true that regular Mass-goers are also supporters of the Church's moral teachings?

Prayer

Jesus, we worship you and thank you for the gift of your real presence among us in the Most Holy Sacrament of the Eucharist. May we always imitate the love you have for us in our prayers and acts of charity and service for our brothers and sisters. Amen.

CHAPTER TWENTY-NINE

BUILD STRONG FAMILIES

> *What does the fourth commandment require?* It commands us to honor and respect our parents and those whom God, for our good, has vested with his authority. — COMPENDIUM, 455

The Fourth Commandment focuses on the duties of children to their parents as well as the responsibilities of adult children to their elderly parents. It also deals with all who exercise authority, such as teachers, judges, leaders, and all who hold governing authority.

A man and a woman, bound by their marriage vows, together with their children, form a family. God is the author of marriage and the family. The institution of the family exists before all other institutions — such as the state, schools, businesses, artistic communities, and the media. These other institutions should nurture marriage and the family, and they should responsibly conserve its growth and development.

The Christian family is the school of virtues. When parents and children practice faith, hope, love, and the cardinal virtues, the family realizes its ideal as a "domestic Church." A faith-based family witnesses the loving communion of Father, Son, and Spirit.

A story from Linda and Richard Eyre's *Teaching Your Children Values* demonstrates the importance of the cardinal virtues in family life. Little Jonah's father knew that his child craved attention. Dad knew that all too often parents tend to give attention to negative behavior and ignore positive deeds. The inclination to expend energy on correcting faults needs the balance of approving good behavior. Jonah's dad caught his son doing something right and let him know it with a touching result:

One Sunday afternoon I looked up over the newspaper I was reading and noticed a rather distraught, unhappy look on the face of six-year-old Jonah.

"What's wrong, buddy?"

"Oh nothing."

"You sure?"

"Yeah."

I looked back to the newspaper, but my mind wasn't on the words. I was thinking of yesterday afternoon — the soccer game — and the miserable little kid who had called Jonah a "klutz."

I put down my paper and pulled Jo up on my knee.

"You know, buddy, I've been thinking a lot lately about some things you are extra good at."

"Me?"

"Yes. Do you know that you're incredibly good at being friendly to other kids."

I went on telling him things he was extra good at. The list included "making the baby laugh," "saying your *r*'s clearly," and "remembering to brush your teeth." Jonah's whole demeanor changed before my eyes. His posture changed, his expression changed to a glow. His eyes took on a sparkle. He soaked up the praise like a dry sponge.

"Dad, let's write these down!"

"Write what down?"

"Write down those things I'm good at." He wanted to preserve them, to lay claim to them.

"Where?" I said, glancing around for a piece of paper....

"Here," he said, "right here on my hand. Write with your pen on my hand the things that I'm good at."

And I did. And he didn't wash his hand until his mom made him.[46]

A strong family is the secret of a strong culture. In developed regions and countries — such as Europe, Canada, the United States, Australia, and Japan — the family is declining and is under increasing stress. In fact, twenty nations — including Russia, Japan, Poland, Austria, Italy, and Greece — report a negative population growth.[47] Healthy societies demand healthy families. Only lively families have the generational memory of the past and a commitment to future family life. They actually make history and honor it. Academics prize progress, but how can progress happen when certain opinion makers undermine birthrates, the fidelity of couples, and the essential role of religion in the raising of children?

The current fashion of secularism wants to strip the presence of God from education and entertainment (other than to mock faith), and from moral norms in business, the workplace, and sports. Many court decisions are also taking the "oxygen" out of the family, thus choking the life out of the culture. Wherever family life is dying, so also is the future of a culture dying. Is it possible for life to continue without the religious dimension? The Church tries in every way to help the family resist attacks on its existence and integrity because the family is the fundamental "cell" of the "body" of a society and its culture.

The cause for the decline and fall of empires is similar: a loss of faith-based morality and the collapse of the family. Trust and confidence in God form the basis of wholesome family life. When trust and faith in Christ is weakened, so also is the mutual respect and confidence among family members imperiled and then replaced by chaos, division, and breakdown.

"Nazareth is the school where we begin to understand the life of Jesus. It is the school of the Gospel.... Oh, how I would like to become a child again and to return to this humble and yet sublime school of Nazareth! How I would like to repeat, so close to Mary, my introduction to the genuine knowledge of the meaning of life and to the higher wisdom of divine truth! But my steps are hurried, and I must take leave of my desire to pursue here this never-ending education in understanding of the Gospel."[48]

— POPE PAUL VI

Disciplined love has always been the best-kept secret of vibrant family life. But once the members buy into the fashion of mutual suspicion, relationships are rusted, prayer becomes a foreign language, active participation in parish worship fades, faith falters, hope vanishes, and love is among the ruins.

Discussions of family are essentially tied up with marriage. The state of marriage and the state of family are

A Bill of Rights for the Family

In 1981, Pope John Paul II wrote:

"The Synod Fathers mentioned the following rights of the family:

1. the right to exist and progress as a family, that is to say, the right of every human being, even if he or she is poor, to found a family and to have adequate means to support it;

2. the right to exercise its responsibility regarding the transmission of life and to educate children; family life;

3. the right to the intimacy of conjugal and family life;

4. the right to the stability of the bond and of the institution of marriage;

5. the right to believe in and profess one's faith and to propagate it;

6. the right to bring up children in accordance with the family's own traditions and religious and cultural values, with the necessary instruments, means, and institutions;

7. the right, especially of the poor and the sick, to obtain physical, social, political, and economic security;

8. the right to housing suitable for living family life in a proper way;

9. the right to expression and to representation, either directly or through associations, before the economic, social, and cultural public authorities and lower authorities;

Continued on next page

Continued from previous page

10. the right to form associations with other families and institutions, in order to fulfill the family's role suitably and expeditiously;
11. the right to protect minors by adequate institutions and legislation from harmful drugs, pornography, alcoholism, etc.;
12. the right to wholesome recreation of a kind that also fosters family values;
13. the right of the elderly to a worthy life and a worthy death;
14. the right to emigrate as a family in search of a better life."[49]

part of a single reality. Empowering marriage is a blessing for the family.

Restoring a Christian vision of family is a godsend for a marriage. The Fourth and Sixth Commandments, together with the implications of the Sacrament of Matrimony, are the elements of the God-based vision for both marriage and family. The cultural roadblocks to marriage, such as easy divorce or laws that impoverish couples, need to be reformed. Cultural obstacles to faith growth in children require vigorous exposure and a demand for change. Pro-marriage and pro-family customs, laws, public opinions, and media self-scrutiny should be protected from the present unacceptable attitudes that weaken married couples and rob children of their religious birthrights.

Changing hearts is the prelude to changing the world. It's been done many times before. History is prologue. Empires fall, but new cultures are born. It will happen again. Jesus tells us confidently, "I am with you always, to the end of the age" (Matthew 28:20) and "I have conquered the world!" (John 16:33).

For Reflection

1. What role does family prayer play in your household?
2. How well does your family participate regularly in parish Sunday worship?
3. What is your judgment about the use of authority in schools, at work, and in local, state, and national government? What recommendations would you make for improvement?

Prayer

Father in heaven, creator of all,
you ordered the earth to bring forth life
and crowned its goodness by creating the family of man.
In history's moment when all was ready,
you sent your Son to dwell in time,
obedient to the laws of life in our world.
Teach us the sanctity of human love,
show us the value of family life,
and help us to live in peace with all men.

— FROM THE ALTERNATE OPENING PRAYER FOR
THE FEAST OF THE HOLY FAMILY

CHAPTER THIRTY

THE DIGNITY OF LIFE

> *Human life must be respected because it is* sacred. *From its beginning human life involves the creative action of God and it remains forever in a special relationship with the Creator, who is its sole end. It is not lawful for anyone directly to destroy an innocent human being. This is gravely contrary to the dignity of the person and the holiness of the Creator. "Do not slay the innocent and the righteous" (Exodus 23:7). —* COMPENDIUM, *466* (EMPHASIS IN ORIGINAL)

The many moral issues related to the Fifth Commandment would require a book of their own. In this chapter, the defense of life in general, and abortion and euthanasia in particular, are highlighted. While unable to give due attention to murder, suicide, war, and the death penalty, we believe the "great principle" to respect life will be honored by our readers on such issues.

Politically, many are beguiled by the argument that abortion should be safe and rare. The secular culture expects us to be persuaded by the many other positions that it claims contextualize abortion — such as social justice for the poor, the immigrants, and the unwanted in society, as well as the quest for peace and economic progress. In other words, favor abortion to get rid of abortion. Behind this smokescreen is the invitation to accept abortion, embryonic stem-cell research, *in vitro* fertilization, prescreening of unborns for abnormalities that would "justify" aborting them, and other related positions dealt with by the Vatican's 2008 document *Dignitatis Personae* ("The Dignity of a Person"). People should not forget that the Church extends Christ's gift of mercy to those who have had an abortion. Project Rachel is a ministry for those mothers who have had an abortion and mistakenly think they have committed an unforgivable sin. Psychologically and spiritually they believe that God will never forgive them. Project Rachel brings God's mercy to them to restore their relationship with our Lord, and offers them counseling and support.

Legalized abortion has already won approval from the U.S. Supreme Court, and euthanasia — called "physician-assisted suicide" — is now legal in Oregon, Washington, and most recently in Montana. To borrow from an old metaphor: The camel's nose is not just in the tent, but the camel itself has entered.

Sometimes we may feel helpless in the face of onslaughts to life, but reason and faith are gifts whereby the secular mentality of our society will be freed from the culture of death. Bernard Nathanson is one example.

In 1945, at age 19, he made his girlfriend pregnant. He told her to get an abortion, which she did. Then he dropped her. Ten years later he made another woman pregnant. This time, having become a doctor, he aborted the child himself. He proceeded to open an abortion clinic in New York City. Through the years, he performed or presided over thousands of abortions.

Then two events affected him so deeply that he changed his mind completely about abortion. In 1968, he was writing a magazine article about the morality of clinic blockades. He went to see the demonstrators, did interviews, took notes, and observed the facts. "It was only then," he wrote in his autobiography, *The Hand of God*, "that I apprehended the exaltation, the pure love on the faces of that shivering mass of people, surrounded as they were by hundreds of New York policemen."[50] They made him wonder about his own behavior and about what motivated them.

The second step in his conversion was caused by the invention of ultrasound. It showed that the being in the womb could suck its thumb and do other human-like things. From that time on, Nathanson abandoned abortions altogether.

In 1984, he premiered a movie, *The Silent Scream*, which showed an ultrasound of a child being aborted. From then on, he embarked on a spiritual search, and he looked for a way to "wash away" his sins. "I felt the burden of sin growing heavier and more insistent,"[51] he said, later sharing his thinking at the time: "I have such heavy moral baggage to drag into the next world that failing to believe would condemn me to an eternity perhaps more terrifying than anything Dante envisioned in his celebration of the redemptive fall and rise of Easter."[52]

Nathanson was helped by Father John McCloskey, a priest based at Princeton University and a well-known adviser to intellectual seekers. Finally, after many years of searching, Dr. Nathanson, at age 69, converted to the Catholic Church. He stood before Cardinal John O'Connor at the baptismal font and renounced forever the world, the flesh, and the devil. "I will be free from sin," he thought. "For the first time in my life, I will feel the shelter and warmth of faith."[53]

God blessed Bernard Nathanson with the gift of faith. To be delivered from the sin of taking the life of the unborn requires a conversion of heart. It is possible to use

The Author of Life

Faith in God means a relationship with the author of life. Faith means accepting the words of Jesus: "I came that they may have life, and have it more abundantly" (John 10:10). Without a serious relationship with God, the defense of life will fade.

reason to stop depriving the unborn of life, as Nathanson did when he saw the sincerity of pro-life witnesses and again when ultrasound convinced him that the being in the womb acted humanly. But finally, it was our Lord who brought him to faith, to trust in his divine reality and his liberating mercy.

Pope John Paul II wrote many life-affirming documents that command our attention, but the one that applies most cogently to our present situation is his extraordinary encyclical *Evangelium Vitae* ("The Gospel of Life," 1995). So pertinent has it been that America's most influential newspaper, the *New York Times*, featured it on its front page and printed it as a "document of record." The pope touched a nerve in American culture that boldly challenged the secular world that wants, for the most part, just the opposite of what he preached. The testimony of Pope John Paul II raised the pro-life discussion to a level that millions in our country can no longer avoid. As he wrote, "All human beings, from their mothers' womb, belong to God who searches them and knows them … who gazes on them when they are tiny shapeless embryos and already sees in them the adults of tomorrow, whose days

Against Physician-Assisted Suicide

In 1995, Judge John T. Noonan, as a member of a three-judge panel of the Ninth Circuit Court, issued an opinion reversing an earlier decision by Judge Barbara Rothstein in *Compassion in Dying v. State of Washington*. The following is a paraphrased summary of his argument:

1. We should not have physicians in the role of killers of their patients. It would perversely affect their self-understanding and reduce their desire to look for cures for disease if killing instead of curing were an option.

2. We should not subject the elderly and infirm to the psychological pressures to consent to their own deaths.

3. We should protect the poor and minorities from exploitation. Pain is a significant factor in the desire for doctor-assisted suicide. The poor and minorities often do not have the resources for the alleviation of pain.

4. We should protect all of the handicapped from societal indifference and antipathy and any bias against them.

5. We should prevent abuses similar to what has happened in the Netherlands, which now tolerates both voluntary and *involuntary* euthanasia.

Note: Catholic moral tradition has always taught that people can discontinue medical procedures that are burdensome, extraordinary, or disproportionate to the outcome. The use of painkillers to alleviate the sufferings of the dying, even at the risk of shortening their lives, is morally permissible so long as death is not willed or intended.

are numbered and whose vocation is even now written in the 'book of life.'"[54]

When John Paul's moral teachings on respect for life (from conception to natural death) become issues in politics, many Catholics get confused because they have never understood that honoring human life from its very beginning is the foundational teaching upon which all the rest depends. The very concept falls on post-modern deaf ears that often are unable to understand rational distinctions or arguments from reason in general.

Not only has reason dimmed among many Catholics and others in our society, but also the light of faith seems to have lost its relevance for them. Why else have over 50 percent of Catholics avoided regular participation in the Eucharist and decided for themselves what they want to believe?

For Reflection

1. How strongly have you defended life in your family, in your parish, in your workplace, and in the voting booth?
2. What happens to a society that tolerates violence?
3. What steps can your family take to establish a culture of life?

Prayer

O LORD, you have searched me and known me.
You know when I sit down and when I rise up;
    you discern my thoughts from far away....
For it was you who formed my inward parts;
    you knit me together in my mother's womb.

I praise you, for I am fearfully and wonderfully made….
My frame was not hidden from you,
when I was being made in secret….
Your eyes beheld my unformed substance.
In your book were written
all the days that were formed for me….
Search me, O God, and know my heart.

— PSALM 139:1-2, 13-14, 15, 16, 23 (EMPHASIS ADDED)

CHAPTER THIRTY-ONE

FAITHFUL LOVE

> Therefore a man leaves his father and his mother and clings to his wife, and they become one flesh.
> — Genesis 2:24

We all know the Sixth Commandment: "You shall not commit adultery." Stated positively it admonishes, "You shall commit fidelity." It is an invitation to staying faithful in marriage, in friendship, and in community. Of course, its principal goal is a loving marital fidelity. The commandment opposes adultery but proposes fidelity. In his teaching on marriage and divorce, Jesus reminds us that God is the author of marriage and that the couple should stay faithful, and that no human being should separate them. When questioned about Moses' permission to divorce, Jesus said Moses responded to their hardness of heart, but that was not God's plan in the beginning:

> "Have you not read that the one who made them at the beginning 'made them male and female,' and said, 'For this reason a man shall leave his father and mother and be joined to his wife, and the two shall become one flesh'? So they are no longer two, but one flesh. Therefore what God has joined together, let no one separate." (Matthew 19:4-6)

The Ninth Commandment supplements the Sixth with a call to inner purity. Jesus says, "You have heard that it was said, 'You shall not commit adultery.' But I say to you that everyone who looks at a woman with lust has already committed adultery with her in his heart" (Matthew 5:27-28). Adultery is having sex with someone else outside of marriage. Adultery is infidelity to one's spouse. It is a sin against the bond of love and one's marriage vow taken in the presence of God and the Church. It breaks one's promise to stay faithful to the beloved. Jesus says that lust for another person in one's heart is already a form of adultery.

One modern couple who are being considered for sainthood because of the fidelity of their marriage bond are the parents of St. Thérèse of Lisieux.

Zélie Guérin (1831-1877) wanted to be a nun but was told she had no vocation. Louis Martin (1823-1894) had hoped to be a monk but was refused because he knew no Latin. They had met a few months before their subsequent disappointments, but they then fell in love and soon married in the Church of Notre Dame at Alençon, in northern France, in 1858.

Zélie ran a successful lace-making business with fifteen employees. Louis was a watchmaker who eventually sold his watch shop to handle Zélie's finances. They had nine children, of whom five girls lived to adulthood. Busy as they were, the parents committed themselves to contemplative prayer, daily Mass, and family prayer. Four of their daughters joined the Carmel at Lisieux, and one daughter entered the Visitation community. Thérèse, the youngest, is one of the most popular of the Church's canonized saints — the Little Flower of Jesus.

Like all families, they had their problems, including a lawsuit, untimely deaths, and the stress of balancing faith, prayer, and business. The parents mourned the deaths of four of their children. They carefully fostered the spiritual lives of their remaining daughters.

Louis and Zélie actively supported the poor, financially and in other ways. Louis was a member of the St. Vincent de Paul Society, dedicated to caring for the poor. Zélie met once a week with her employees to discuss their needs. She nursed her maids when they were sick. The poor often came to their home for food, clothing, and a kind word. Love pervaded their home — love for one another, their friends and relatives, and the poor. They loved Christ in others. No wonder their daughter Thérèse, in discovering her special calling, wrote: "I will be love in the heart of the Church."

Zélie and Louis Martin stayed faithful to each other until death parted them. They based their relationship on a deep prayer life, an awareness of God's presence in their lives, and an unwavering attention to the final purpose of life with God hereafter. They treated each of their girls as unique individuals and trained them in the spiritual ideals they themselves followed. They showed them how to face conflict and pain with faith in God. They involved them in concern for charity and justice for the poor and needy. They witnessed a joyful marriage founded on the love of Christ and were beatified on October 19, 2008, at Lisieux, on Mission Sunday.

"My dearest, I cannot get back to Alençon before Monday; the time seems long to me, for I want so much to be with you. I embrace you with all my whole heart, while awaiting the joy of being with you again…. Your husband and true friend who loves you forever."[55]

— LETTER OF LOUIS MARTIN TO HIS WIFE, ZÉLIE

Chaste living in soul and body is the real way to stay faithful. This requires a discipline of the eyes and of the passions. Modesty protects the mystery of the human person so that we do not exploit one another. Today's TV shows have become increasingly erotic, showing men and women wearing seductive clothing, glamorizing infidelity, and in some cases presenting vivid and explicit sexual passion. If we include pornography, then the corruption is brazen and absolute. When conflicts in a marriage invariably arise, it is necessary to repair the relationship *and* avoid any temptations that arise from television or the Internet.

Studies of love often make the distinction between falling in love and staying in love. Romantic love is filled with satisfying emotions, intense feelings that both attract the lovers to one another and temporarily blind them to faults and pitfalls that lie ahead in the relationship. The stories of stage, screen, poetry, and novels find a treasure trove in this common experience of falling in love. It's a classic case of love being so blind that lovers cannot see. It makes adultery possible in marriages that did not make the transition to disciplined love. It causes couples to forget the counsel they received from wise parents and friends: that true love always includes sacrifice, and to stay connected in the midst of pain, refusing to split in the face of marital challenges. Fall in love, yes. Stay in love, by all means.

One of the major purposes for establishing loving fidelity in marriage is for the needs of children to be nurtured by the life, teachings, and examples of their parents. Married adults should never forget these basic needs of children. Children's mental, physical, and spiritual health requires wholesome parents who give them the love and stability so important for self-confidence, security, and well-founded hope. Our culture has all too many cases of children wounded by divorce.

> "Fidelity in marriage means much more than abstention from adultery. All religious ideas are positive, not negative. Husband and wife are pledges of eternal love. Their union in the flesh has a grace that prepares and qualifies both souls for the union with God.... The passing of time wears out bodies, but nothing can make a soul vanish or diminish its eternal value. Nothing on earth is stronger than the fidelity of a heart fortified by the sacrament of [marriage]."[56]
>
> — Archbishop Fulton Sheen

The culture encourages relationships that undermine legitimate marriage, such as free unions, "trial marriage," and imaginary marriage between same-sex partners. As these behaviors increase, the anarchy in real marriage expands. The false freedom that results misleads people, who are thereby encouraged to seek such "liberation."

For Reflection

1. What do you think is the secret to a long and happy marriage?
2. Why do so many marriages end in divorce?
3. How might the Sixth and Ninth Commandments apply to priests and male and female religious?

Prayer

Blessed are you, God of our Fathers;
praised be your name forever and ever.
Now, Lord, you know I take this spouse of mine,
not because of lust, but for a noble purpose.
Call down your mercy on us,
and allow us to live together to a happy old age.

— ADAPTED FROM TOBIT 8:5, 7

CHAPTER THIRTY-TWO

LOVE AND SOCIAL JUSTICE

> *Wash yourselves; make yourselves clean;*
>   *remove the evil of your doings from before my*
>   *eyes;*
> *cease to do evil,*
>   *learn to do good;*
> *seek justice,*
>   *rescue the oppressed,*
> *defend the orphan,*
> *plead for the widow.* — ISAIAH 1:16-17

The Seventh and the Tenth commandments have, at their core, love of neighbor and social justice. In biblical terms, love and justice are two forms of one reality: the need to treat others with compassion and include respect for everyone's human dignity as well as a social conscience. The Seventh Commandment's concern for stealing is about more than theft, though that is wrong. It speaks also to the wider reality of social justice in many forms. It is the core reality behind the Church's social teachings. The various social encyclicals since Pope Leo XIII's landmark *Rerum Novarum* (On Capital and Labor, 1891) constitute a charter of social justice with a broad agenda.

From these storied documents come such themes as: a living wage for a family, government responsibility for the poor, no peace without justice, awareness of the financial needs of developing countries, compassion for immigrants, the excesses of capitalism and socialism, and the Church's prophetic responsibility on behalf of the poor and oppressed. A spirituality without a social conscience is flawed.

The life of Archbishop Oscar Romero (1917-1980) is the story of a modern martyr for social justice. Born in El Salvador, Romero was ordained in 1942 and was sent to Rome for further studies. After his return to El Salvador, he served as a parish priest in Anamoros and later at the cathedral. Made a bishop in 1970, he eventually became archbishop of San Salvador in 1977.

Up to this time, he worked mainly with the prosperous families of his country. Once he became archbishop, he heard from his priests about the *campesinos*, the thousands of extremely poor workers on the great landed estates of the wealthy. He began to leave his privileged surroundings and go out to meet the poor. In doing so, he realized the dreadful conditions in which they lived. He visited the priests and nuns who worked closely with the oppressed and argued for justice on their behalf. Soon he became aware of murders of some of those who spoke up to the rich and to the government, pleading for a living wage for the workers and better living conditions for their families.

Romero then went public, writing columns in newspapers and giving radio talks and powerful sermons to alert his country and the world of the vast injustices suffered by his people. He angered the ruling class, the military, the government, and even some fellow bishops. He told everyone, "There can be no Church unity if we ignore the world in which we live." Soon he received threats against his life. He said, "If I am killed, my blood will be the seed of freedom."

On March 21, 1980, he was offering the 6:45 p.m. Mass in one of the small chapels in his cathedral. As Romero lifted the chalice containing Christ's holy Blood, a lone gunman in the back of the chapel lifted a high-powered rifle and shot one bullet at the archbishop. Romero fell to the floor, soaked in blood. The Eucharistic Blood of Jesus mingled with his blood. Romero had supported the human rights of the poor. He opposed the violence and repression aimed at the oppressed. He often said, "I beg you. I beseech you. Lay down your guns." He also implicitly prayed, "Here is my body. Lord, take it. Here is my blood. Jesus, take it." God heard his prayer. Archbishop Romero died in the cause of justice for his people.

"May this Body immolated and this Blood sacrificed for Mankind nourish us also, that we may give our body and our blood over to suffering and pain, like Christ — not for self, but to give harvests of peace and justice to our people."[57]

— ARCHBISHOP OSCAR ROMERO
(UTTERED SECONDS BEFORE HIS DEATH)

The Tenth Commandment complements the Seventh by addressing possessions and our means of obtaining them — money. Jesus often talked about money. He praised the widow for giving out of her tiny resources in contrast to those who gave from their abundance and mistakenly soothed their consciences. She gave till it hurt. He condemned, in a parable story, the unjust manager who begged mercy for his debt but treated cruelly another man who owed him a much smaller amount and pleaded for mercy and time to pay it. Jesus challenged the rich young man who wanted to know how to be saved. Jesus told him to keep the commandments. The young man replied that he had done so since his childhood. Looking at him with deep love, Jesus said that if he wanted to be perfect he should sell all he had and give the money to the poor and come follow him. The rich young man looked very sad as he walked away from Christ, for he was very wealthy.

One reason that Jesus spoke so much about money is that "the love of money is the root of all evils" (1 Timothy 6:10, RSV). All financial panics and extreme financial collapses can be traced to greed in some form, as the meltdown that began in 2008 affirms. Greed occurs at all levels of society and, sadly, sometimes even in the Church. Credit card debt afflicts millions of households, while business and bank debt overshadows the world economy. In the movie *Wall Street*, the main character addresses his stockholders with the soothing but detestable statement, "Greed is good." But greed is bad. Just see how it affects everyone, from the worker to a captain of industry to the so-called financial wizards, from everyone on Wall Street to everyone on Main Street and, tragically, to Side Streets. As always, the poor suffer the most when greed breeds a collapse.

The Opposite of Greed

What virtue would prevent greed from seducing so many? Temperance. What modesty does for responsible sexuality, temperance provides for responsible attitudes about money. Temperance restrains the impulse to consumerism, supplies the will to save rather than recklessly spend, provides the contentment to live within one's means, helps refuse the lure of easy money, and shows us how to appreciate that "less is more."

Matthew's Gospel places Christ's judgment of the nations in the middle of Holy Week, just two days before the Passion. Faced with his forthcoming redemptive death, Jesus delivered a sermon on the standards whereby we will be saved or refused salvation. Artful as always, Jesus paints the picture we will one day see:

> "When the Son of Man comes in his glory, and all the angels with him, then he will sit on the throne of his glory. All the nations will be gathered before him, and he will separate people one from another as a shepherd separates the sheep from the goats, and he will put the sheep at his right hand and the goats at the left. Then the king will say to those at his right hand, 'Come, you that are blessed by my Father, inherit the kingdom prepared for you from the foundation of the world; for I was hungry and you gave me food, I was thirsty and you gave me something to drink, I was a stranger and you welcomed me, I was naked and you gave me clothing, I was sick and you took care of me, I was in prison and you visited me.'" (Matthew 25:31-36).

Jesus teaches us that if we want to go to heaven, we should see him and serve him in the needs of the hungry, the thirsty, the stranger, the naked, the sick, or the prisoner. It's a very personal approach. While sending a check is important, personally feeding hungry people, clothing the homeless sitting on the cold pavement, sitting by the side of the sick and comforting them, going to a jail and treating the prisoner as Christ himself, and welcoming strangers into your community are the times you will find Jesus. Conversely, if you fail in these basic ways of meeting Christ by helping others, you know where you are going. The unusually harsh words of Jesus are clear: You will go to eternal punishment.

These ways of meeting people in need train us in divine love. Just picture Mother Teresa with two of her nuns walking through the streets of the poor and lifting dying men and women from the gutters, taking them home, feeding them, clothing them, washing them, touching them with a care that flows from the throne of mercy. This is the cure for greed. This is the message of justice in action. This is the kiss of love and justice.

For Reflection

1. What do you think of the idea that "the money you give to the poor is theirs, not yours"?
2. The Church teaches that there is a universal destination of the goods of the earth, meaning that all people should benefit from the fruits of creation. What needs to be done to make that happen?
3. Why do most people think that "money is the root of all evil," instead of "*the love of money* is the root of all evil"?

Prayer

Our heavenly Father, all peoples of the earth are your children, and all are our brothers and sisters. Enlighten our minds and hearts with the fire of your love, and give us the wisdom and courage to do your will in ending all divisions and war, and to work toward a world of justice, love, and peace. We ask this in Jesus' name. Amen.

CHAPTER THIRTY-THREE

THE WAY AND THE TRUTH

> *Let the lying lips be stilled*
> *that speak insolently against the righteous*
> *with pride and contempt.* — PSALMS 31:18

The Eighth Commandment's words forbid telling lies — lies that injure a person's reputation, lies that cripple community, lies that rob little old ladies of their income, lies that cause hatred. As the *Catechism* explains, "This moral prescription flows from the vocation of the holy people to bear witness to their God who is the truth and wills the truth" (CCC, 2464).

One of the high points of John's Last Supper narrative deals with truth. Jesus asks the apostles to trust him and not to lose heart when they see the troubles that will befall him. He predicts that he will go to his Father's house and prepare a place for them. He reminds them that he has taught them the way to where he is going. Thomas, wired with doubt, says they do not know where Jesus is going. How can they know the way?

Jesus replies, "I am the way, and the truth, and the life" (John 14:6). Usually a teacher claims he has the truth, but never says he *is* the truth. Jesus goes beyond an ordinary teacher by proclaiming he is Truth.

If a student believes a certain teacher has truth, he or she accepts it from him and moves on. If the student believes the teacher is the Truth, he or she may well follow him and become a disciple. Jesus personalized Truth in an exceptional way not possible for a creature. By using the biblical "I AM," Jesus reveals his divine identity as well as incarnating truth in his humanity. Truth is a key to his identity. Denying truth means denying a crucial fact about Christ and blocks our relating to him in a proper manner.

The issue arises again during his dialogue with Pilate, who questioned him about being a king. In Pilate's eyes, if Jesus claimed such a title, he would then become a political rival — not an approved puppet king like Herod, but a self-appointed royal rebel leader, which Rome could never tolerate. Jesus rejected Pilate's error and told him that his kingdom is a universe of truth. Jesus let him know that he came to bear witness to the truth. Pilate's famous answer was, "What is truth?" (John 18:38).

In that hour, facing eternal truth, Pilate proved himself to be a relativist. His world was a universe of conflicting popular opinions. He needed agile skills to navigate the sea of opinions that protected Rome and his job in Palestine. His next move made the point. He gave the people the chance to free either Jesus or a terrorist, Barabbas. The people's voice yelled for Barabbas. Jesus must die. To add insult to injury, Pilate then washed his hands, as though this would exempt him from any responsibility for the killing of Jesus. That's what relativism can do to an innocent man-God.

It is not hard to arouse the hatred of liars. It is more difficult to clear the fog of a culture that has adopted relativism that denies the reality of truth and supports the squishy dictatorship of popular opinion — today whitewashed as "political correctness."

> "There is one thing a professor can be absolutely certain of: almost every student entering the university believes, or says he believes, that truth is relative."[58]
>
> — ALLAN BLOOM

Pope Benedict XVI has been drawing the world's attention to this breakdown in the advanced cultures of the developed nations. He has famously said that it is a "dictatorship of relativism" that tolerates every kind of opinion while it denies the reality of truth. While this theory commands the allegiance of the cultural leaders, it is also part of the lived experience of a good portion of everyday society. The version that prevails among many members of our Church is the "Cafeteria Catholic," the pick-and-choose parishioner who has lost the valid seriousness of our faith and has decided to create his or her own religion. The nondenominational mega-churches attract many such Catholics.

Pope Benedict constantly calls everyone back to the use of reason that can know the truth, the natural law that reflects the divine law of truth, and faith as a legitimate source of the knowledge of truth. And, of course, he is even more ardent in retelling the truths of divine revelation so essential for our full personal development as well as our salvation.

Today, the prevalence of doubt, a preference for ambiguity, and a huge discomfort with the concept of absolute truth have gradually taken center stage. This confuses people of goodwill who are committed to truth as the North Star of their journey in dark times.

Truth eventually wins out. The "big lie" of the Nazis was defeated and proved wrong. The false promises of

Holy Wisdom Dispels Deceit

God gave Pope John XXIII (1881-1963) the gift of holy wisdom. For thirty years, as archbishop and then cardinal, Giovanni Roncalli served in the Church's diplomatic corps. After that, he became patriarch of Venice and finally pope. When asked what he learned about being an administrator, he said: "See everything, correct a little, and forget the rest." He brought to his work the shrewd peasant wisdom he learned on his family farm in Sotto il Monte. A reporter wanted to know how many work at the Vatican. Pope John smiled and said, "About half of them."

One of his favorite expressions when faced with pressures was *"Piano, piano"* (Softly, softly), which in English is something like the expression "Take it easy." Yet, anxious to speed up the preparations for the Second Vatican Council, even he expressed his frustration to a friend who said, "Why don't you give stronger orders?" Thinking about it, he grumbled: "I'm only the pope around here."

John XXIII's wisdom was a mix of patience, humor, trust in God, and transparency. He was a blend of the country pastor and the sophisticated diplomat. He loved people, and the world returned the favor.

In his speech at the opening of Vatican II, Pope John stressed the continuity of the Church's teachings and fidelity to revealed truth, while urging the bishops to find fresh and attractive ways of expressing this ancient heritage of the Church. In his defense of truth, he was never harsh — but like St. Francis de Sales, he placed truth between love and hope so that he could feed a world hungering for God. His wisdom put deceit on the defensive and made enormous room for Christ, the Truth.

communism were never delivered, and it, too, is in the dustbin of history. In time, truth will trump relativism. The Church proclaims that truth is more than an abstraction for philosophers to debate. Instead, truth is a Person, Jesus Christ, Son of the living God. His truth is a form of love and trust-building. It is a solid rock upon which our relationship with Christ flourishes. It is a thumbs-up for a nation searching for uplifting love that is not just another mirage. The more people refuse to settle for anything less than honesty, real sincerity, and the gold standard of truth, the quicker the specter of relativism will collapse under its failed promises.

For Reflection

1. Why is the devil called the Father of Lies?
2. Why might we say that our culture is experiencing a crisis of truth? How does your faith and prayer help you stand up for truth?
3. Since Scripture is the Word of God, how does it strengthen you in your commitment to truth?

Prayer

May God grant me to speak with judgment,
and to have thoughts worthy of what I have received;
for he is the guide even of wisdom
and the corrector of the wise.
For both we and our words are in his hand,
as are all understanding and skill in crafts.
For it is he who gave me unerring knowledge of what exists,
to know the structure of the world and the activity of the
    elements.

— WISDOM 7:15-17

CHAPTER THIRTY-FOUR

AVE MARIA

> The "splendor of an entirely unique holiness" by which Mary is "enriched from the first instant of her conception" comes wholly from Christ: she is "redeemed, in a more exalted fashion, by reason of the merits of her Son" (LG 53, 56). The Father blessed Mary more than any other created person "in Christ with every spiritual blessing in the heavenly places" and chose her "in Christ before the foundation of the world, to be holy and blameless before him in love" (cf. Eph 1:3-4). — CCC, 492

We come to the end of this discussion of Truth, Love, and Longing with a meditation on Mary. She is a powerful link between us and her beloved Son, Jesus. She makes heaven seem accessible when we feel distant from God. She takes away our timidity before the divine and helps us accept intimacy with the Holy Spirit.

One way we can stay in touch with Holy Mary — who is our Holy Mother, and who loves praying for us and our needs — is through the Miraculous Medal.

The story began in 1830 at a convent in Paris. Sister Catherine Labouré (1806-1876) was awakened from sleep and led by hand by an angel to the chapel. There she had a vision of our Blessed Mother. This experience was followed by several others. In the last appearance, Mary showed Catherine the images of a medal. The front showed Mary with her hands stretched in a gesture of welcome. Around her, at the edge of the medal, were the words, "O Mary, conceived without sin, pray for us who have recourse to thee."

On the back of the medal was a large "M" for Mary. The "M" was surmounted by a bar and cross. Beneath the "M" were two hearts, one pierced by a sword in memory of the prophecy of Simeon that Mary's heart would be wounded by a sword, a prediction that came true at the Crucifixion. A crown of thorns rested on the other heart, recalling the mockery of Christ as a king just after the scourging at the pillar. Circling these images were twelve stars, recalling the vision of the woman in chapter twelve of the Book of Revelation, which many interpret as a scriptural picture of Mary.

Mary then instructed Catherine to have a medal struck according to these images, promising great graces to all its wearers. Catherine shared these visions with her confessor, and with the permission of the archbishop of Paris, the first medals were produced and distributed in 1832. Many remarkable favors followed, and in a relatively short time use of the medal spread throughout the whole Church. Countless millions of these medals have been made for devotional use, both in Catherine's time and in our own.

Sister Catherine Labouré secured a promise from her confessor not to reveal her identity as the visionary. She requested a transfer to an obscure convent in the south of France, where she lived the rest of her days. Nine months before she died, she revealed her story to the superior of the convent. She was canonized by Pope Pius XII on July 27, 1947.

People usually wear the medal on a chain around their neck. Sometimes it is tucked into a wallet or purse, or even a car's glove compartment. Other followers of this devotion hang it from a car's rear-view mirror, or otherwise display it in many other ways.

The medal illustrates our teaching about the Immaculate Conception, especially in the prayer that honors Mary as "conceived without sin" and begs the Immaculate to pray for us. That devotional approach was marvelously effective in helping vast numbers of Catholics to understand this privilege of Mary, and in 1854 Pope Pius IX formally declared this teaching a dogma of the faith.

Theology and Devotion Meet in Mary

One outstanding example of the link between theology and devotion occurred at the conclusion of the Council of Ephesus (431), which declared that Mary was the Mother of God, the *Theotokos*. This had been the belief of the Church from the beginning. The birth stories of Jesus in Matthew and Luke were crystal clear that the Virgin Mary conceived Jesus by the power of the Holy Spirit. The bishops at Ephesus were reaffirming the ancient faith of the Church, much to the delight of the lovers of Jesus and Mary. The first public act that evening was a joyous candlelight procession through the streets of Ephesus, praising Christ for honoring Mary to be his mother. In other words, popular piety smoothly linked a doctrinal truth with a celebratory parade. Popular devotion contributes positive feelings to a personal identification with the truths of faith, while doctrine, Scripture, and liturgy — in mutual agreement — assure the reliability of the truths celebrated.

Finally, through the intercession of Mary, so many divine favors were received by those who had the medal, it became popularly known as the Miraculous Medal.

When the bishops at Vatican II were discussing *Lumen Gentium*, the document on the Church, they debated whether to have a separate one for Mary or to include her in this constitution. At the time, there was apprehension among some bishops about popular piety regarding Mary. They decided it needed to be guided through the doctrine about the Church, which is what they did. However, a brief comment about some excesses in Marian devotion led to unintended consequences. Just after the council, public devotion to Mary declined. Pope Paul VI hastened to correct this by giving Mary a new title: "Mother of the Church."

Gradually, a solid and exuberant devotion to Mary returned. In large part, this was due to the extraordinary devotion to Mary by Pope John Paul II. Going against the custom that forbade lettering on the papal coat of arms, he placed an "M," for Mary, on it. His motto was *Totus Tuus* — "Totally Yours." His enthusiastic love of Mary was contagious and affected the universal Church positively. Pilgrimages to the great shrines of Mary grew even larger. The Rosary continues to attract a vast multitude. Despite the tendency to name baby girls after movie stars, the most popular name for baptisms remains Mary. The arrival of millions of Hispanics in the United States has also brought their love of Our Lady of Guadalupe, along with huge festivals on her feast day, December 12. Greater enthusiasm for the celebrations of our Holy Mother Mary in the liturgy has become more prominent, as well as connecting devotion with the scriptural and doctrinal truths contemplated at worship.

> "Mary is a woman of faith: 'Blessed are you who believed,' Elizabeth says to her (cf. Lk 1:45). The *Magnificat* — a portrait, so to speak, of her soul — is entirely woven from threads of Holy Scripture, threads drawn from the Word of God. Here we see how completely at home Mary is with the Word of God, with ease she moves in and out of it. She speaks and thinks with the Word of God; the Word of God becomes her word, and her word issues from the Word of God. Here we see how her thoughts are attuned to the thoughts of God, how her will is one with the will of God. Since Mary is completely imbued with the Word of God, she is able to become the Mother of the Word Incarnate."[59]
>
> — POPE BENEDICT XVI

What is happening is a synergy — a mutual interaction of devotion, liturgy, and doctrine — that includes the creed and morality. This development is a recovery of the way the Church of the Fathers integrated the elements of faith. Theirs was an age in which the bishops were usually theologians as well as leaders in worship and catechetical pastors. They were often pictured holding the Bible in their laps. It would never have occurred to them to specialize the components of the wealth of the faith. There was ultimately a seamless garment of the creed, sacraments, morality, prayer, and devotion.

The Power of the Hail Mary

When Cardinal John O'Connor (1920-2000) was chair of the bishops' Committee on Pro-Life Activities, he would celebrate Mass at the Basilica of the National Shrine of the Immaculate Conception, in Washington, DC, on the evening of the March for Life. One year, in front of the shrine, pro-choice protestors walked in a circle with their posters and chants. It was rumored that a number of protestors had infiltrated the pews to interrupt the Mass.

The cardinal spoke just before the service and said that he knew that some people in the congregation were prepared to cause a commotion during the worship. He said, "I know you are here. I want you to know I love you, but I disagree with your beliefs. I ask you not to interfere with our service out of respect for God and this holy place."

Then after the reading of the Gospel, as the cardinal began his homily, eight people in the front pew stood up and unfurled a big sign that proclaimed, "Keep Abortion Legal." EWTN was televising the Mass. Knowing this, the protestors exploited this visual opportunity. After this, screams of blasphemies arose from all parts of the shrine. The sound was reminiscent of the demons recorded in Scripture. Then, with quiet dignity, the People of God began reciting the best-known and most revered Marian prayer, the Hail Mary. Miraculously, the shouting suddenly died away. Our Holy Mother, through her sons and daughters, silenced the sacrilegious yells.

Members of the city's SWAT team had been briefed earlier and had been invited to help with security, which they did by escorting the sign bearers quickly from the church. The Mass continued without further incident.

For Reflection

1. What Scripture accounts about Mary appeal to you most and for what reason?
2. How would you describe your relationship to our Holy Mother Mary?
3. If you have made a pilgrimage to a Marian shrine, what was it like? What would you advise others to do to promote devotion to Mary?

Prayer

The *Memorare*

Remember, O most gracious Virgin Mary, that never was it known that anyone who fled to thy protection, implored thy help, or sought thy intercession was left unaided. Inspired by this confidence, I fly unto thee, O Virgin of virgins, my mother. To thee do I come, before thee I stand, sinful and sorrowful. O Mother of the Word Incarnate, despise not my petitions, but in thy mercy hear and answer me. Amen.

ACKNOWLEDGMENTS

Notes

1.　Thomas Merton, adapted from *The Seven Storey Mountain* (New York: Harcourt Brace Jovanovich, 1948), 108-110.

2.　Pope Paul VI, *Evangelii Nuntiandi* (On Evangelization, 1975), *http://www.vatican.va/holy_father/paul_vi/apost_exhortations/documents/hf_p-vi_exh_19751208_evangelii-nuntiandi_en.html*, 41.

3.　St. John of the Cross, *Ascent of Mount Carmel,* Book II, Chapter 20.

4.　Matthew 11:28 from NRSV; Psalm 89:34 from *The Psalms: A New Translation* (England: The Grail, 1963, 1991), 160.

5.　Thomas à Kempis, *The Imitation of Christ*, translated by Leo Sherley-Price (London: Penguin Books, 1952), 205.

6.　Chaim Potok, *The Gift of Asher Lev* (New York: Ballantine Books, 1997), 151.

7.　Pope Benedict XVI, *Jesus of Nazareth* (New York: Doubleday, 2007), xxi.

8.　Pope John Paul II, homily for the canonization of Edith Stein (October 11, 1998), *http://www.vatican.va/holy_father/john_paul_ii/homilies/1998/documents/hf_jp-ii_hom_11101998_stein_en.html.*

9.　Robert Louis Wilken, *The Spirit of Early Christian Thought* (New Haven, CT: Yale University Press, 2003), 106-109.

10.　Irving Stone, *The Agony and the Ecstasy* (New York: Doubleday, 1961), 538.

11.　Pope John Paul II, *Crossing the Threshold of Hope* (New York: Alfred A. Knopf, 1994), 23. Emphasis in original.

12.　Blessed Columba Marmion, *Christ, the Life of the Soul* (Colorado Springs, CO: Zaccheus Press, 2005), 432.

13.　Thomas à Kempis, op. cit., 209.

14.　Caryll Houselander, *A Rocking-Horse Catholic* (Westminster, MD: Christian Classics, 1988), 112.

15.　Charles J. Healey, S.J., *Modern Spiritual Writers: Their Legacies of Prayer* (New York: Alba House, 1989), 119.

16.　Houselander, op. cit., 138.

17.　Dietrich Bonhoeffer, *Letters and Papers From Prison: New Greatly Enlarged Edition* (New York: Touchstone, 1997), 360-361.

18. St. Gregory Nazianzen, *Catechism of the Catholic Church* (CCC, 684).

19. Henri De Lubac, *The Splendor of the Church* (San Francisco: Ignatius Press, 1986, 1999), 54.

20. Catholic Online, *Prayer for the Church #2, http://www.catholic .org/prayers/prayer.php?p=584*.

21. Alfred McBride, O.Praem., *Images of Mary* (Cincinnati: St. Anthony Messenger Press, 1999), 13-14.

22. Thomas à Kempis, op. cit., 57.

23. Zenit news agency, Elizabeth Nguyen Thi Thu Hong (Address of Cardinal Van Thuan's Sister at Congress), *http://www.zenit.org/article-22959?l=english* (June 19, 2008).

24. Ibid.

25. Pope Benedict XVI, *Spe Salvi* (On Christian Hope, 2007), *http:// www.vatican.va/holy_father/benedict_xvi/encyclicals/documents/ hf_ben-xvi_enc_20071130_spe-salvi_en.html*, 32.

26. Thi Thu Hong, op. cit.

27. Pope Benedict XVI, papal homily for the International Eucharistic Congress in Quebec (June 22, 2008), *http://www.vatican .va/holy_father/benedict_xvi/homilies/2008/documents/hf_ben-xvi_ hom_20080622_quebec_en.html*.

28. Ibid.

29. Pope John Paul II, *Catechesi Tradendae* (On Catechesis, 1979), *http://www.vatican.va/holy_father/john_paul_ii/apost_exhortations/ documents/hf_jp-ii_exh_16101979_catechesi-tradendae_en.html*, 54.

30. Bishop Arthur Serratelli, "The Recovery of the Sacred," *http:// www.patersondiocese.org/page.cfm?Web_ID=2237*.

31. Fulton Sheen, *The Priest Is Not His Own* (San Francisco: Ignatius Press, 2005), 230-236.

32. Pope John Paul II, *Dives in Misericordia* ("Rich in Mercy," 1980), *http://www.vatican.va/holy_father/john_paul_ii/encyclicals/documents/ hf_jp-ii_enc_30111980_dives-in-misericordia_en.html*, 15.

33. Timothy Keller, *The Reason for God: Belief in an Age of Skepticism* (New York: Dutton, 2008), 172. Emphasis in original.

34. Anthony De Stephano, *Ten Prayers God Always Says Yes To: Divine Answers to Life's Most Difficult Problems* (New York: Doubleday, 2007), 91-92. Emphasis in original.

35.   Romano Guardini, *The Lord* (Washington, DC: Regnery, 1988), 130.

36.   Pope John Paul II, *Salvifici Doloris* (On the Christian Meaning of Human Suffering, 1984), *http://www.vatican.va/holy_father/john_paul_ii/apost_letters/documents/hf_jp-ii_apl_11021984_salvifici-doloris_en.html*, 10, 26. Emphasis in original.

37.   See *The Rites* (New York: Pueblo Publishing, 1983), 8-13.

38.   Archbishop Hélder Câmara, quoted by Vicky Kemper and Larry Engel in *Sojourners* (December 1987), 12.

39.   Pope John Paul II, *Letters to My Brother Priests*, 1979-1999 (Chicago: Midwest Theological Forum, 2000), 104.

40.   Quoted in Francis P. Friedl and Rex Reynolds, eds., *Extraordinary Lives: Thirty-Four Priests Tell Their Stories* (Notre Dame, IN: Ave Maria, 1997), 95.

41.   Catholic Online, *http://www.catholic.org/prayers/prayer.php?p=1997*.

42.   C. S. Lewis, *Surprised by Joy: The Shape of My Early Life* (Orlando, FL: Harcourt, 1955), 228-229.

43.   Pope Benedict, homily for the closing of the Twenty-Fourth Italian National Eucharistic Congress (May 29, 2005), *http://www.vatican.va/holy_father/benedict_xvi/homilies/2005/documents/hf_ben-xvi_hom_20050529_bari_en.html.* Emphasis in original.

44.   Pope John Paul II, *Ecclesia de Eucharistia* (On the Eucharist in Its Relationship to the Church, 2003), *http://www.vatican.va/edocs/ENG0821/_INDEX.HTM,* 8. Emphasis in original.

45.   Pope John Paul II, *Dies Domini* (On Keeping the Lord's Day, 1998), *http://www.vatican.va/holy_father/john_paul_ii/apost_letters/documents/hf_jp-ii_apl_05071998_dies-domini_en.html,* 39.

46.   Linda and Richard Eyre, *Teaching Your Children Values* (New York: Simon and Schuster, 1993), 33-34.

47.   Matt Rosenberg, "Negative Population Growth: 20 Countries Have Negative or Zero Natural Increase," *http://geography.about.com/od/populationgeography/a/zero.htm.*

48.   Pope Paul VI, adapted from an address at the Basilica of the Annunciation in Nazareth (January 5, 1964), *The Pope Speaks* (Vol. 9, No. 3; 1964), 284-286.

49.   Pope John Paul II, *Familiaris Consortio* (On the Role of the Christian Family in the Modern World, 1981), *http://www.vatican*

.va/holy_father/john_paul_ii/apost_exhortations/documents/hf_jp-ii_
exh_19811122_familiaris-consortio_en.html, 46. Cf. CCC, 2211.

50. Bernard N. Nathanson, M.D., *The Hand of God: A Journey from Death to Life by the Abortion Doctor Who Changed His Mind* (Washington, DC: Regnery, 1996), 192.

51. Ibid., 187-188.

52. Ibid., 195-196.

53. Bernard Nathanson, as quoted in "Bernard Nathanson's Conversion," by Julia Duin, *Crisis* (June 1996).

54. Pope John Paul II, *Evangelium Vitae* ("The Gospel of Life," 1995), *http://www.vatican.va/holy_father/john_paul_ii/encyclicals/documents/hf_jp-ii_enc_25031995_evangelium-vitae_en.html*, 61.

55. Paulinus Redmond, *Louis and Zélie Martin: The Seed and the Root of the Little Flower* (London: Quiller Press, 1995), 124.

56. Fulton J. Sheen, *Three to Get Married* (New York: Scepter Publishers, 1951), 131.

57. Archbishop Oscar Romero, as quoted on *http://luterano.blogspot.com/2006/07/top-10-romero-quotes.html.*

58. Allan Bloom, *The Closing of the American Mind* (New York: Simon and Schuster, 1987), 25.

59. Pope Benedict XVI, *Deus Caritas Est* ("God is Love," 2005), *http://www.vatican.va/holy_father/benedict_xvi/encyclicals/documents/hf_ben-xvi_enc_20051225_deus-caritas-est_en.html*, 41.

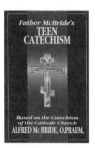
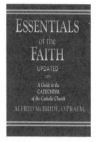
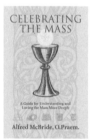